Object Technology
Made Simple

BY MORY BAHAR

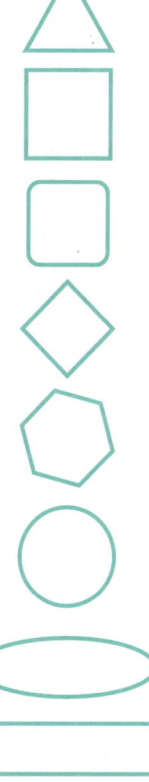

Simple Software Publishing

Copyright © 1996 by Mory Bahar. All rights reserved, including the right of reproduction in any form, in whole or in part. For information, write to Mory Bahar, Simple Software Publishing, 2220 Middle Road, East Greenwich, Rhode Island 02818.

All company or product names are trademarks or registered trademarks of their respective holders.

Published by Simple Software Publishing.

Printed on recycled paper. Printed and bound in the United States of America.

ISBN: 0-9652457-0-5

Dedication

This book is dedicated to my father, whose wit and wisdom will always be my goal and inspiration.

Contents

Foreword	ix
Acknowledgments	xi

Chapter 1
Objects Demystified 1
    Why All This Fuss About Object Technology? 1
    Key Attributes of Object Technology 2
    Let's Get Simple! 2
        Example: A Home Stereo System 2
    So What's New About this Object Stuff? 5
    Introducing... an Object! 6
        Example of an Object: Recipe for a Bloody Mary! 6
    Methods and Messages 7
    Objects Behave 9
    Examples of Software Objects 10

Chapter 2
Objects in Time — How Did We Get Here? 13
    The Evolution of Software Development Technology ... 13
        In the Beginning, There Was Business 13
        The Awakening 14
        Feudal Times (The Medieval Era) 15
        The Renaissance 16
        The Contemporary Period 18
        Modern Times 19
        The New Frontier 19
    In Summary.... 20

Chapter 3
In Pursuit of Buzzword Proficiency 23
    The Power of the Buzzword 23
    Key Buzzwords in Software Development History 23
    Buzzwords and Object Technology 25

Chapter 4
Objects, the Software Industry and You 31
    What It Means to the Industry 31
    Objects Do It Naturally! 32
    What It Means to Your Organization 33
    So Why is It so Hard to Get Computers To Do What We Want? 35
    People are Object-Oriented ... Programmers are Not! (Yet) 39

Chapter 5
So Let's Develop an Object-Oriented Application! (Follow Me to a Nearby Saloon!) — 41
    Identifying the Objects — 41
    Identifying Object Behavior — 42
    Defining the Messages — 42
    Developing the Application — 43
    A Real-World Application: Looks Like a Bar! — 44
    Let's Generalize.... — 45
    The Promise of Object-Oriented Development — 46

Chapter 6
Wrapping Your Arms Around Objects (How to Get Started) — 47
    How to Get Started with Object Technology — 47
    Smoothing Out the Changes — 49
    Barriers to Adopting Object Technology — 49
    Management Commitment — 51

Chapter 7
Object Methodologies, Tools and Players — 53
    The Importance of Modeling — 53
    The Methodology Madness! — 54
    Understanding Methodologies and Tools *(Parlez-vous français?)* — 54
    Evaluating the Methodologies — 58
    Who Are the Big Players in Object Technology? — 60

Chapter 8
What Lies Ahead? — 63
    And Finally, the Conclusion.... — 66

Index — 69

Recipe for a World-Class Bloody Mary! — 73

About the Author — 75

Ordering Information — 78

Foreword

When I first gave the talk "Object Orientation Made Easy" in San Jose, California, in 1992, I was very gratified by the response. Audiences started asking for copies of my presentation, and I don't think this was entirely due to the popularity of the Bloody Mary recipe (see page 6, if you can't wait). People were eager to take the slide copies back to their organizations and show them how the concept of objects *can* be made simple — that is, explained in an understandable and entertaining manner. Just as objects represent real-world items, we can explain them in simple, real-world language. That came as a surprise to many people.

Of course, there were skeptics. (This book even makes skepticism easy, as I've included a skeptic for you. He's my shadow personality, the little man who stands at the bottom of the page and comments on my comments. Since he was such a popular part of the presentation, it seemed only natural to include him in the book.) But the skeptics usually left convinced, and ready to think about the next step while they were enjoying their Bloody Mary.

Since 1992, I've given the "Object Orientation Made Easy" presentation to a few thousand people around the world. You might say that I found it much easier to keep attracting new audiences than to develop a new presentation. The important factor, though, is that the new audiences kept on coming, as more and more software developers and managers thought about the tremendous promise and potential productivity and quality benefits offered by object technology. Finally, I realized that there were many, many more people out there who wanted to know, and that the best way to reach them was to set down my presentation in the form of a book. So here we are.

You don't need any previous knowledge of object-oriented terminology or methodologies to use this book. We'll take you on a colorful shortcut through the forest of concepts and confusion, the wise words and the buzzwords. As my shadow personality says on page 1, "Whatever you do, keep it simple."

We will.

Mory Bahar
March 1996
Providence, RI
U.S.A.

Acknowledgments

This book is the result of the education, assistance and guidance that I have received over the years from a long list of friends and associates. One could say that it's just another example in my career where I get the credit for the contributions of so many others!

I'd like to thank Jim Lally, who was the first to suggest creating such a book.

I'd like to thank a number of friends and associates who reviewed the book and offered me numerous suggestions. Among them are David Butler, Dave Dayton, Bruce Donath, Dr. Hans Hermans, Patricia Hood, Steve Manson, Lou Mazzuchelli, Scott Miller, Don Millers, Herb Morton, Carl Olofson, Don Page, Terri Savidge, Peter Stephinson, Ronnie Thompson and Arthur Vogel.

I also wish to acknowledge the creative and artistic work of Bob Seal and Paul Gaj, who produced the illustrations and the cover, respectively. In particular, I want to express my appreciation to Cheryl Walsh who produced all the artwork for the original slide presentation *Object Orientation Made Easy*.

I wish to thank Mohammad Batmanglij for his valuable advice, Ron Imbriale for his support, Gwynne Jamieson for her endless enthusiasm and Maureen Monaghan for her assistance in managing the production of this book. I'd also like to raise my glass to Scott Reiter, who helped me fine-tune the recipe for a world-class Bloody Mary!

And finally, my very special thanks goes to Ann Waterman, who transformed my questionable spoken and written English into its current understandable and proper form, and whose vision, creativity and energy helped to bring this project to a reality. This book is a direct product of her dedication and professionalism.

Objects Demystified

Recommended background music for this chapter:
Dvorak's *New World Symphony*

Why All This Fuss About Object Technology?

Take a lobster, a piano, a toaster and a cowbell, and what have you got? Other than an oddly furnished room, or the elements of a very unusual garage sale, you have *things*. Items. Or, to use another word, objects. When we read these words, we get a mental picture of the item — perhaps not the same mental picture, but still we know what the object is and what, if anything, we can do with it. You may have never thought of a lobster as an object, but view it as an item on a menu or a tourist attraction of New England, and it becomes one. Your fifth-grade teacher becomes an object if we're listing things you loved (or didn't) about your early years. So does something less tangible, such as a reservation if you're planning a visit to a very popular restaurant. So what does all this have to do with the latest in software development technology? Everything!

Object technology is far more than a new buzzword or even a new trend. It's a fundamental change in the way we develop software. Before the advent of object-oriented development techniques, we humans had to see the world as the computers did in order to program. We had to be immediately concerned with intricacies, interfaces, unique languages and many lines of code. Our data and procedures were kept completely separate, and we only had to hope that they came together successfully in the end. With object technology, we finally have the opportunity to interact with computers the way we want: in terms of real-world, recognizable entities. Objects!

As humans, we don't like to think about the intricacies involved in the objects we use. To us, technology is best when it's invisible. When I turn on my stereo system, I want it to play music; I don't want to have to know all about the internal electronics, the cables and connections, or the

"Whatever you do, keep it simple!"

semiconductor theory behind each component. Similarly, when I start my car, I want to know that it will get me to my destination. I'm not interested in the internal workings of the engine, the spark plug timing or the fuel injection complexities. The same is true when we develop software: we'd rather just know how to use a piece of software; that it works; and where to call if it doesn't. Object technology promises to bring us much closer to that goal.

Key Attributes of Object Technology

To understand the benefits of object-oriented software development, we need to begin with some key attributes. These are:

1. Modularity
2. Real-world correspondence
3. Loose coupling
4. Incremental delivery
5. Reuse

That may seem complicated. However, because the goal of this book is to keep it simple, and because I don't want you to yell at me like my shadow personality at the bottom of the page, I'll explain these attributes using a very simple example: a home stereo system.

Let's Get Simple!

Example: A Home Stereo System

Suppose that you and I each want to create our own custom audiovisual system. We go to a store (or several), select some speakers, an amplifier, a TV and a VCR, and then take them home and connect them. Each of us may have chosen different brands and features according to our preference and our budget, but we've both created a working system. Now, let's see what that means in terms of our five attributes of object technology.

"You said this was going to be simple. This stuff doesn't look simple to me!"

Modularity

In an audiovisual system, every element is **modular**, which gives me lots of options. I can take a subset and build a different kind of system, or I can replace my VCR when a better model comes on the market. If I decide I want to outblast my neighbor's stereo, I can exchange my speakers for huge bassboomers. And if something breaks, it's easy to tell which piece needs to be fixed or replaced.

Real-World Correspondence

Each entity in the audiovisual system has a meaningful, **real-world purpose** that's easy to explain. The speakers broadcast sound, and the VCR records and plays back audiovisual signals. It's much simpler to explain the role of a speaker, a TV or a VCR than the role of a transistor, capacitor or resistor inside it!

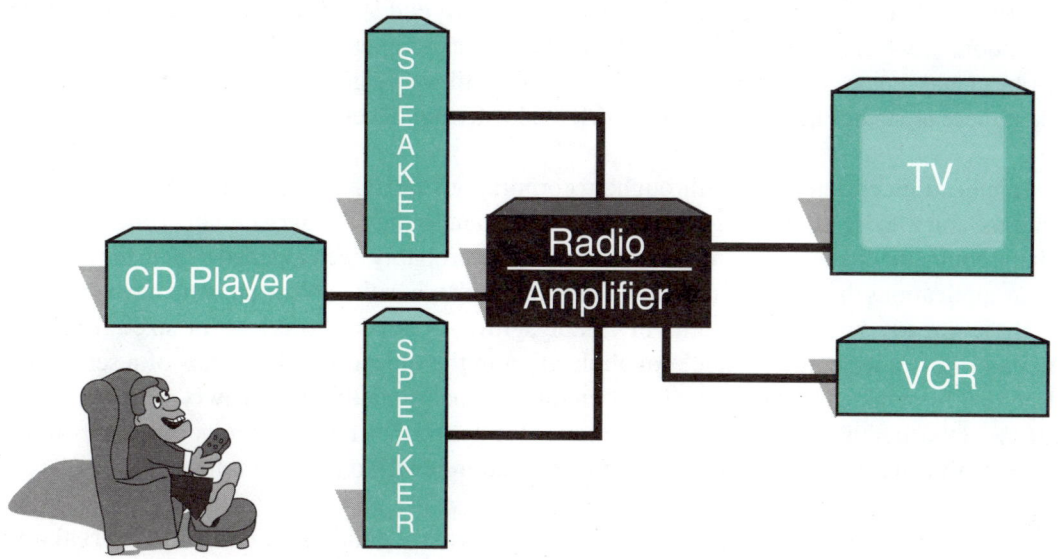

Example: A Home Stereo System!

Loose Coupling

The amplifier I bought will work beautifully with my system or with hundreds of others. This means that the modules of the system are **loosely coupled** — that is, the modules don't require one another to be a specific brand or type in order to work together. When we change modules, the connecting cables can stay the same. This, of course, is made possible through standards and the cooperation and compliance of the various vendors.

Incremental Delivery

If I can't afford all the components I want today, I can buy the items I want most and then add to the system later. I can also review the system at any point along the way, and change it if the neighbors become too angry, or if it no longer meets my needs. This is **incremental delivery**.

Reuse

The amplifier I selected is a part of my system, but it will also work with yours, and my neighbor can borrow it if his loud parties destroy his. The same is true for a speaker, or for any of the other components we chose — so, we can say that the original developer of each piece has created an object that can be **reused** in many different scenarios.

With this simple example, we've just examined the most important attributes of object technology. The promise of object-oriented development is that we can select objects and create a specific application, or we can choose other objects and create a completely different one. We can remove one object and replace it with a new one, and so on, until we've got the system we want. Now, let's look at these attributes in terms of object-oriented software development.

Most applications currently in use throughout corporations and the government are giant, monolithic creations, and they're often as rigid and change-resistant as they are gargantuan. Touching just one variable could invalidate the entire system, and they've probably been touched *a lot* in the past. These are the applications that leave you tempted to call in sick when they blow up. And have you noticed that these already huge applications invariably grow — never shrink! — in size? **Modularity** certainly offers a welcome change! An application in the object world consists of a set of clearly defined, self-contained building blocks, or modules. When something goes awry with the system or with one of the modules, we can much more easily locate and then repair or replace the faulty module. That doesn't cause the application (and your frustration level) to keep growing.

How do we identify these modules? That's easy — **they correspond to something in the real world:** for example, a customer, a product or a cash deposit. We model these modules after things that exist in our business.

And how do we put these modules together to create an application? Well, easily, because they're very **loosely coupled**. This allows us to replace one module without changing any interconnections or interfering with the other modules' operation. Changing, adding or replacing modules won't cause the edifice to come tumbling down. It's because of the loose coupling that we can do all this; the fate of one module does not determine the fate of another.

Modularity and loose coupling also let us take advantage of **incremental delivery**. Combining the modules gives us a basic level of functionality, and as we add more modules we get additional capabilities. Incremental delivery is very important because it lets us demonstrate continuous progress — to our boss, to the end-users, to the customers and to our own team of developers. People just don't like to see two years pass before we come back with something to show them. (Neither does the company's Chief Information Officer, whose tenure may turn out to be less than two years!) Incremental delivery also lets us change our minds — or change the system, if our needs have changed — in a much more cost-effective manner.

Now here comes the biggie: one of the greatest benefits of object technology is **reuse**. In simple terms, reuse means putting together an application using software previously designed and developed by someone else. Today, unfortunately, even those programmers and analysts brave enough to want to reuse software generally have little success in finding software that's reusable.

A real-world object (such as a stereo speaker, for example) is designed once and then manufactured thousands of times; but in software, much too often we develop an application, deploy it once, and then spend the rest of our professional lives trying to maintain it. What's more, not even our colleagues within our own organizations would consider using part of it in their applications. Sadly, today's standard procedure for software is to constantly engineer, design and reinvent the wheel. We keep winding up back where we started! But the good news is that with object technology, we, too, can design an item once and then manufacture it (i.e., deploy it) in thousands of different programs or applications. Because the individual modules are self-contained and loosely coupled, we can use them again in other applications. In creating a vast array of tested, high-quality, *reusable* pieces of software, we not only save development time, but also have a much more reliable product. MIS managers may not be terrifically interested in manufacturing their software modules literally thousands of times, but they'll certainly welcome the day when 80% of their application's functionality can be purchased off-the-shelf!

So What's New About This Object Stuff?

By now you're probably realizing that these attributes aren't really all that new. True! We've seen manifestations of every one of these attributes in some form with previous software development tools, conventions and techniques. And we've had self-contained procedures in software development for a long time — for example, in operating system functions (such as date/time routines that are invoked in many applications), subroutines and shared libraries. Object orientation began as a programming technique that was the logical successor to the structured programming techniques of the past. Object development significantly shifts the focus to up-front analysis and design as opposed

"I thought object technology was all new. This is just formalizing good principles that have been evolving over the years."

to coding; but this, too, could be said of structured methods and CASE tools. *What's new,* though, is *the formality, the discipline and the commitment,* facilitated by new languages; together these ensure that every piece of software we develop is adhering to these attributes and principles, allowing us to derive all the inherent benefits. What's also new is the degree to which we can reuse software — *80% or more of the application,* versus the 10 - 20% we may have had in the past.

Introducing... an Object!

Now we're ready to move to a more technical definition of a software object.

> An **object** is a grouping of data and logic to represent a real-world item.

"Grouping" is the key word here. The data is grouped together with the logic that operates on it, creating one unit of software. The data won't get us very far without the logic, and vice versa. To illustrate, let's use a very desirable real-world object, ***the recipe for a Bloody Mary.***

Example of an Object: Recipe for a Bloody Mary!

Ingredients:

4 oz.	Crushed ice	2 oz.	Vodka
6 oz.	Tomato juice	1/8 tsp.	Salt
1-1/2 oz.	Lemon juice	1/8 tsp.	Freshly ground pepper
1 tsp.	Worcestershire sauce	1/8 tsp.	Minced garlic
4 dashes	Tabasco sauce	1	Celery stalk
1 tsp.	Minced horseradish	1	Lemon slice

Directions:
Mix the tomato juice, lemon juice, vodka, horseradish, garlic, ice, worcestershire and tabasco sauce. Add pepper. Add salt to taste. Shake well. Strain and pour into a tall glass. Insert celery stalk. Add lemon slice on rim and serve.

In this recipe (which, by the way, has been extensively tested over the years, so please enjoy), the ingredients are the data and the directions correspond to the logic. The logic operates on the data to give us the desired outcome: a tasty Bloody Mary!

But first, imagine for a moment how unnatural it would be to keep the recipe in two separate binders. This means that in order to make this drink we'd have to refer to two binders, one listing the ingredients and the other containing the instructions. This violates our expectations since we're used to seeing these things on one page, and it's also something of a nuisance. Now, let's further consider how strange it would be if we always had to have two bartenders, one to put the ingredients on the counter and another to mix them up. With this scenario, a lot of things could happen to prevent us from getting the drink we want. Perhaps the first bartender has run out of lemon juice. To fill the void, he substitutes vinegar, but the

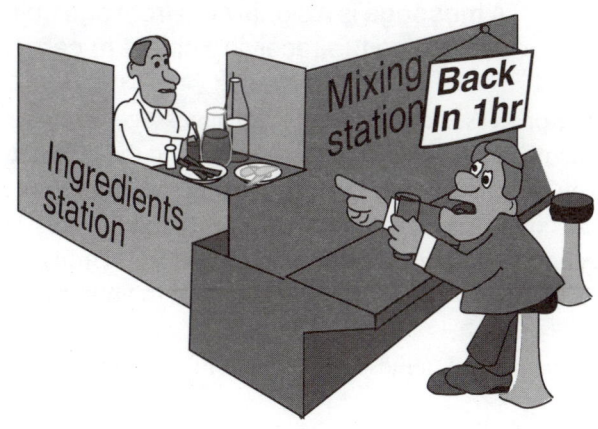

second bartender has no reason to stop making the drink since he's concerned only with the process, not the ingredients. If you're thinking that it's absurd to separate the ingredients (data) from the directions (logic) in this way, consider this: *that's exactly how most software is developed today* — and why object technology is such a tremendously important new development. (We'll return to this very important issue in Chapter 4.)

Keeping in mind the attributes of object technology, here's another way to define an object:

> An object is a self-contained, identifiable, reusable software component that represents a real-world item.

"Self-contained" here means that the data and logic necessary for an object to carry out its purpose are contained within that object.

Methods and Messages

An object-oriented approach gives us much greater confidence in the result because the data and the logic are always together as part of the same object. To explain how this works, we need to introduce two more concepts, "method" and "message."

> A **method** is a service that an object provides, or a task performed by an object.

In our Bloody Mary example, the method corresponds to the directions, without which the drink won't get made. In software development, a method can be a function, a procedure or a subroutine.

> A **message** is a signal sent from one object to another, requesting a service (i.e., requesting the receiving object to carry out one of its methods).

The process is a complete cycle: a message is sent to an object; methods operate on the data within that object; and the result is sent back to the originator. To visualize this process, picture an e-mail you've sent to a colleague, requesting something you need to do your job. You are the sending object, the colleague is the receiving object, and the message is your request. The method is the specific action you want the colleague to perform. Unlike the real world, however, in the world of object technology you always get a response to your message!

To be precise, a message is the combination of both the request and the response.

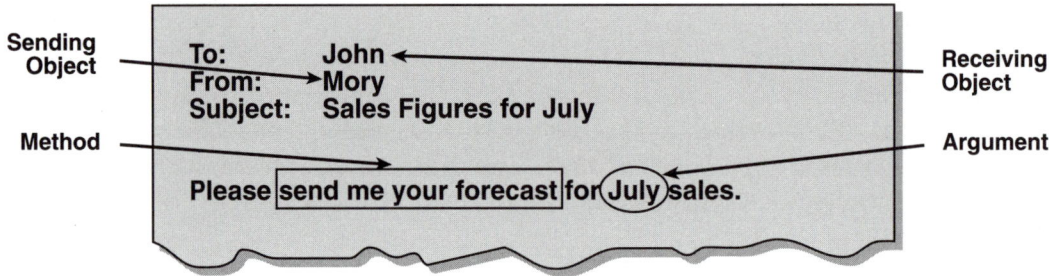

Example of a Message: An E-Mail

To further explain methods and messages, let's go to a larger example, using a factory as our object. The factory contains raw materials (data) and a lot of machinery and people (methods) that operate on them to produce finished goods. The customer (sending object) transmits an order (message) to the factory (receiving object) for some goods. The factory produces the requested material and sends it back to the customer, thus completing the *message*. The message has included both the request (the order) and the response (the fulfillment of that order).

It's important to note that the customer has no interest in what the factory workers and the machinery actually do to produce those goods, only that the finished product is delivered. In software, the details of the process are equally unimportant to the object. Its concern is getting the job done. All the complexity associated with what happens inside the factory (object) to produce the finished goods (desired service) is hidden from the customer (requesting object). This level of modularity, packaging and flexibility allows the object-oriented software developer to deal with complexity much more effectively.

An object can have many methods, but a method can generally belong to only one object. There's no need to duplicate or copy a method (procedure or function) into multiple places (programs) in a system.

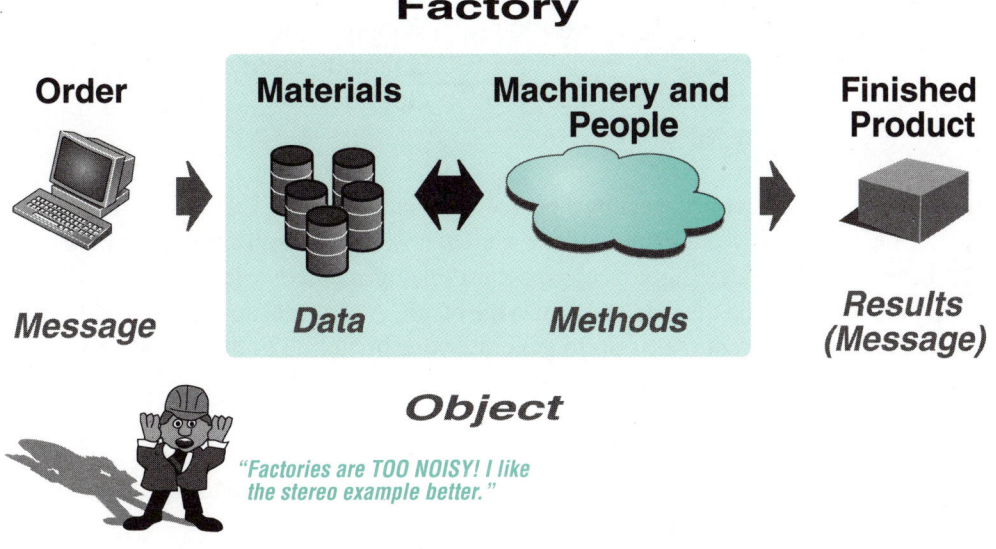

An Object is Like a Factory!

Objects Behave

Objects are valuable to us because they behave. Or, to put it another way:

> The services provided by an object are called its **behavior**.

The purpose of an object is to provide a service to other objects; this is its behavior. Messages request a desired behavior, and methods implement it. To figure out an object's behavior, we observe the messages that go in and out of it. To request a specific behavior, other objects (via a message) invoke (by name) the method producing that behavior.

Examples of Software Objects

For instance, companies maintain vast amounts of data about us as employees. To our company, we have a name, perhaps an employee number, definitely a social security number, a hire date and a salary. Here's an example for an object called Employee:

Object	**Data**	**Method**
Employee	Name	Get name
	Social security number	Print resume
	Address	Calculate salary
	Date of hire	Get address
	Pay rate, ...	

One type of message to this object, sent by a payroll application, might be, "Here's a social security number. Give me this employee's name, address and salary." The payroll system can then issue your paycheck, based on the object Employee's response, using methods (get name, get address and calculate salary) to operate on the data and return the result. A different application could have used the same object (but a different message) to generate your invitation to the company picnic. Here's an example for an object called Part:

Object	**Data**	**Method**
Part	Part number	Get part description
	Description	Place order
	Minimum order quantity	Reserve
	Quantity on hand, ...	

For a machine part, the data might be "part number" and "description." Methods might be "place order" or "reserve." A message sent to this object might be "Reserve a gross of this item." We can illustrate these examples with the following table. Note that a message is composed of the object identifier to which it is addressed; the name of the method that implements the desired behavior; and some arguments or input/output variables.

"It sounds like the only interesting thing about an object is its behavior. I can't believe I said that."

Messages:	Service Being Requested	Object Being Addressed	Input Variable or Argument	Output (Result)
	Get name	Employee	Social security number	Name
	Reserve	Part	Part number, quantity	(Reservation of the part)

In a computer language, the format for these messages might look like:

    Get_Name (Employee, SSN, Name)
    Reserve (Part, Part#, Quantity)

We've now seen some basic object-oriented terminology made simple. Just as we have names for all these aspects of object technology, we also have a name for all these names. We call them buzzwords, and mastery of them is important in order to fully appreciate this new technology. The concept of buzzwords is so overpowering that we could devote an entire chapter to them. In fact, we will. To get to this immediately, skip ahead to Chapter 3. But for those who like to see "the big picture," I invite you to proceed to Chapter 2 for a lighthearted look at how all these marvelous things came about.

"Hmm.... Object, method, message. Are these all the buzzwords you know?"

Object Technology Made Simple 11

Objects In Time — How Did We Get Here?

Recommended background music for this chapter:
the theme from *2001: A Space Odyssey*, or Strauss's *Also Sprach Zarathustra*

The Evolution of Software Development Technology

Objects today are like the transistors and microchips of yesteryear: an essential technological advancement without which time — as we software professionals know it — would have stood still. With the power and affordability of hardware and software being orders of magnitude beyond that of just ten years ago, you can imagine what kind of a milestone we're talking about.

Comparing object technology to the software development of the past is like comparing an integrated circuit (IC) to a vacuum tube. Not only was it a radical departure from what came before, but a completely new paradigm. It suddenly changed all the rules! That's why some organizations have perceived roadblocks in adopting object technology. Whereas the previous enhancements in software development were incremental, progressing relatively easily down the road from one stage to the next, object technology called for us to jump off that road and take another route entirely. That new road turns out to be a superhighway, sending us speeding ahead toward tremendous benefits — but for us to understand where we are now, it helps to understand where we've been.

In the Beginning, There Was Business

So how did this all come about? First we need to look at why any software development comes about: people need to make their business tasks easier. Or they need to improve their key processes, or gain a competitive advantage. To accomplish that (i.e., to develop that automated solution), software developers need easy-to-use software products that give them better productivity, cost effectiveness, quality and reliability. End-users have come to have boundless *expectations* about the systems they use, and this is the reason for the ongoing advancements in software development technology: the need to keep up with user expectations (i.e., business requirements). One may argue that software technology has *never* kept up with user expectations, but it still deserves credit for driving the continuing cycle of need and technological advancement. We can all be grateful for that.

The Beginning

First, There were Hardware Switches... (the 0's and 1's)

Machine Language

E4F1
F000
A1B5

Then Binary States Grouped Into Digits and Instructions... and Software was Born!

The key business requirements and user expectations from software development teams were for automated capabilities that would help them do their jobs faster; reduce their cost of doing business; improve the quality of their work; give them a competitive advantage; and promote innovation and new product or service development. (Software developers, in turn, have similar expectations from their software development tools and technologies.)

And so the software development technologies advanced to meet those end-user and developer expectations. These advances have always taken the form of *allowing us to define our needs at a higher level of abstraction* — that is, to remove ourselves further and further from the nuts and bolts (or 0's and 1's) of how computers work toward a simple way of telling them what we want them to do. Let's take a look at how this process has evolved over the years.

The Awakening

The prehistory of software (from the late 1940s through the 1950s) can be summed up in one word: **hardware**, the essential element that can be compared to the primeval soup. Swimming around in this mire were binary states — hardware switches of ons and offs, or 0's and 1's — waiting patiently for the moment that would change the course of history. Finally, it happened: the 0's and 1's were combined into meaningful sequences, creating digits, instructions and programs. A precise sequence of digits corresponded to each precise machine instruction — and, appropriately, this way of specifying our needs became known as machine language. Thus, software was born! But it was a primitive and helpless form of technology, because although the hardware could exist independently of the software, the reverse was not true. The software hadn't yet crawled firmly onto the shore.

The missing element, of course, was a more human-oriented language. Machine language represented an early form of abstraction, but at a very low level. Needless to say, human programmers began to find such conversation annoying, so the language progressed to a higher level called assembly language, using some limited alphanumeric expressions (such as "LDA" for "Load Register A", instead of "4FF1"). Certainly, this was an improvement, but it was still very limiting. The languages and programs were hard to learn, and they lacked any kind of uniformity. Worse still, each of those assembly instructions was tied to a specific machine!

Man Learns to Speak

Feudal Times (The Medieval Era)

It didn't take long — only a decade or so — for the engineers to realize that they didn't want to be dominated by a machine, so they chose instead to be dominated by a language. With the advent of common, standard languages such as COBOL and FORTRAN (and many others that didn't fare as well and have since been consigned to the halls of museums), software developers — as they had now become — could express their requirements at a still higher level of abstraction. For example, they could use one COBOL statement that translated to 20 different machine instructions, with every compatible compiler on every machine able to translate it! Of course, there were the inevitable feuds over which language to use, and which version of which language, but at least these third-generation languages (called 3GLs) no longer required an intimate knowledge of the hardware. Evolution was speeding along now, with developers using a language that was a little closer to their own.

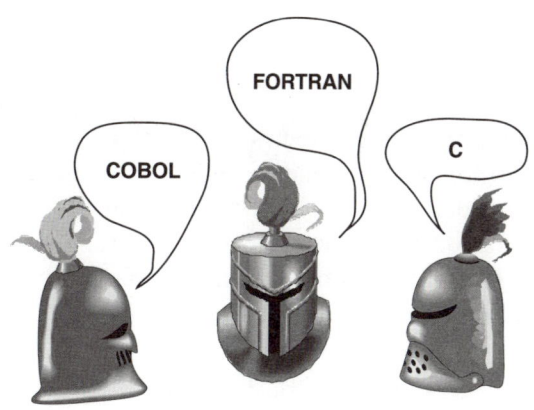

Standards-Based, Higher-Level Languages are Born!

So, apart from the feuds, what was the problem? To keep up with the end-users' growing demands, the 3GL programs grew ... and grew ... and got out of control, creating a medieval monster that still haunts us: *complexity*.

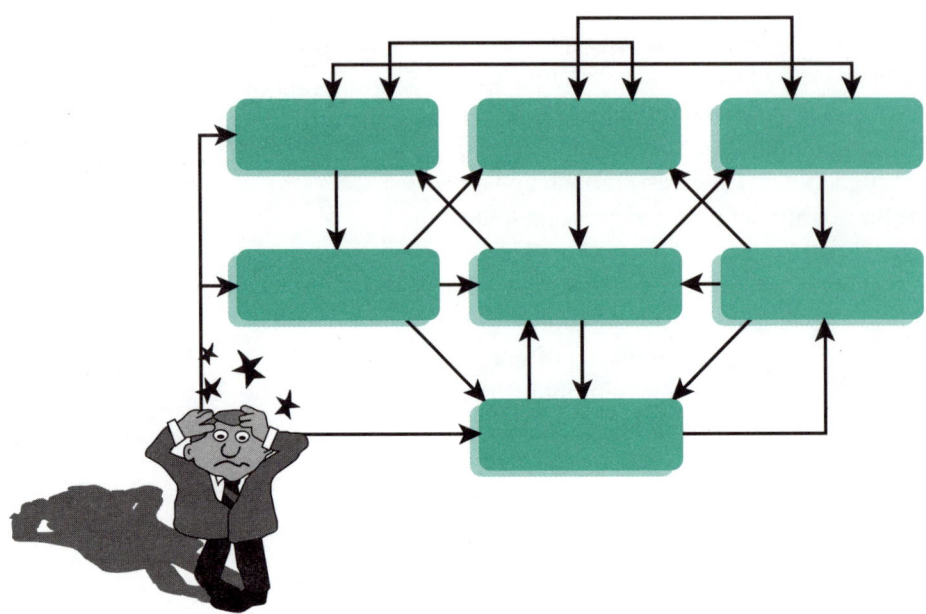

Complexity!

The programs were just too big, too complicated and too difficult to change. It took too much time to produce them, and the result was often a tangled, unstructured mass of spaghetti code. Meanwhile, major industries were becoming more and more dependent on their computers, and their expectations for computers and computer-based solutions were increasing — far beyond the state of technology. (Note that most of the systems from this era are still in use today!)

The Renaissance

Fortunately, this dark era soon gave rise to a new order, a sort of cultural reawakening, as the industry gurus said, "Let there be structure!" Soon there emerged the famous figures of the Renaissance. Dijkstra. Chen. Yourdon. DeMarco. Constantine. The chaos of feudal times began to ebb with the advent of diagrams, techniques and methodologies. Step-by-step "cookbook" approaches gave coherence and repeatability to software develop-

ment. Because developers wanted to communicate their requirements at a still higher level of abstraction, another group of higher-level languages was born. Called fourth generation languages (4GLs), these made programming much simpler, as one 4GL statement could correspond to multiple COBOL statements. Data dictionaries and database management systems made data handling a lot easier. It was all very nice.

"Let There Be Structure!"

Of course, none of this would've affected our lives so dramatically except for one important fact: *the world at large was becoming aware of computers*. From the visible, real-world injection of computers into people's routine tasks (such as booking airline reservations) to the more fanciful depictions of cultural icons (such as the computer-driven universes of *Star Trek* and *2001*), people were beginning to realize what wonderful things computers could do for them. Fueled by the gradual proliferation of personal computers in the home and the workplace, people's expectations began a rapid, upward spiral. And the race was on!

People began to realize and acknowledge that there was a backlog of computer applications waiting to be developed and deployed — and backlog thrived because programmers were too busy trying to maintain their humongous, medieval applications. Sometimes they would try to replace these applications, and they ran into a new problem called *runaway systems* — projects that are eternally over budget and behind schedule. The 4GLs just weren't mature enough to handle the complexity, the volume and the interoperability of the applications. The methodologies were somewhat helpful, but they were difficult to enforce and implement. We needed far more than a methodology to find our way through the maze of charts representing different parts of the system — and there was no way of knowing which of the myriad other charts we'd have to track down and change if we altered even one. With no automated tool support, people soon ran out of wall space to tack up their diagrams!

And thus arrived the Contemporary Period.

The Contemporary Period

We needed help! For a start, we needed to *automate* these methodologies. Fortunately, we now had powerful and affordable PCs and workstations with which to do this — and so along came CASE (Computer-Aided Software Engineering). This was a marvelous breakthrough! CASE harnessed the power of the computer itself to assist in the development of software. CASE tools automated the structured techniques and methodologies of the past and made their use much more practical. Soon we had maintenance tools. Diagramming tools. Modeling tools. Code generation tools. Reverse engineering tools. Requirements traceability tools. Dynamic analysis tools. These gave us pictures representing the different parts of an application and their relationships, and these pictures were quite handy. Automated support for analysis, design, documentation and code generation was certainly welcome, and long overdue! But we still weren't speaking the language of the businessperson, or the engineer, or the accountant; we were expecting them to learn the language of the methodology, the tool and the computer. Real-world entities and business processes just didn't (and still don't) naturally map to these things. The technology also fell short of people's growing expectations in terms of reuse, rapid response to change, coexistence and interoperability of the new software with the old, etc.

It's important to mention that during this period another major revolution in computing took place. As PCs, minicomputers and UNIX platforms became abundant, organizations recognized the economic advantages of transferring some of the workload from their expensive mainframes to these much cheaper machines. This revelation, along with the ease of use of the PCs and minis, resulted in a major movement known as downsizing and client/server phenomena. It's also important to note, however, that client/server, or distributed computing (which I'll talk more about in the next chapter), doesn't actually represent a new way of *developing* application software but rather a new way of deploying it.

At this point, several fundamental challenges in software development still remained: inflexibility; lack of business orientation; hand-crafting (as opposed to using a more predictable, manufacturing-like process); and insufficient reuse. User expectations remained unmet in terms of speed, fulfilling specific requirements, etc.

We were indeed ready for Modern Times — which brings us to the present and the arrival of a new software development technology.

Modern Times

The stage was set for the advent of object technology, which would soon revolutionize software development in the same way that the IC revolutionized electronics.

Modern Times is where we are, and what the rest of this book is all about. But to complete our history of the evolution of software development technology, let's recognize that we're all approaching a New Frontier — the Internet/Intranet Era. Like object technology, this has been around for a while, but it's recently become much more practical, affordable and easily accessible for widespread use.

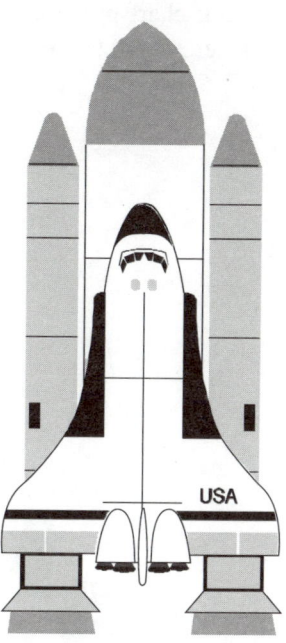

The New Frontier

There has indeed been a rapid emergence of the Internet (i.e., a network of networks of many users), intranet (use of the Internet for internal application within an enterprise), World Wide Web (or WWW for short — a *vast* information resource), HTML (hypertext markup language, with which documents are prepared for the World Wide Web), Java (a C++ based object-oriented programming language aimed at application development for the Internet), and more. These are such important recent developments, and have resulted in such massive confusion and chaos among software developers, vendors and end-users, that they deserve their own book... or two. (Perhaps one by this same author? Just a thought....)

Object technology is certain to remain a key element in realizing the full potential of this new era. As for whether the Internet/Intranet Era will represent a significantly new way of developing software rather than just a new way of using it — well, the jury's still out on that one.

In Summary....

The following chart provides a summary of the key phases in the ongoing (and never-ending) software development technology evolution.

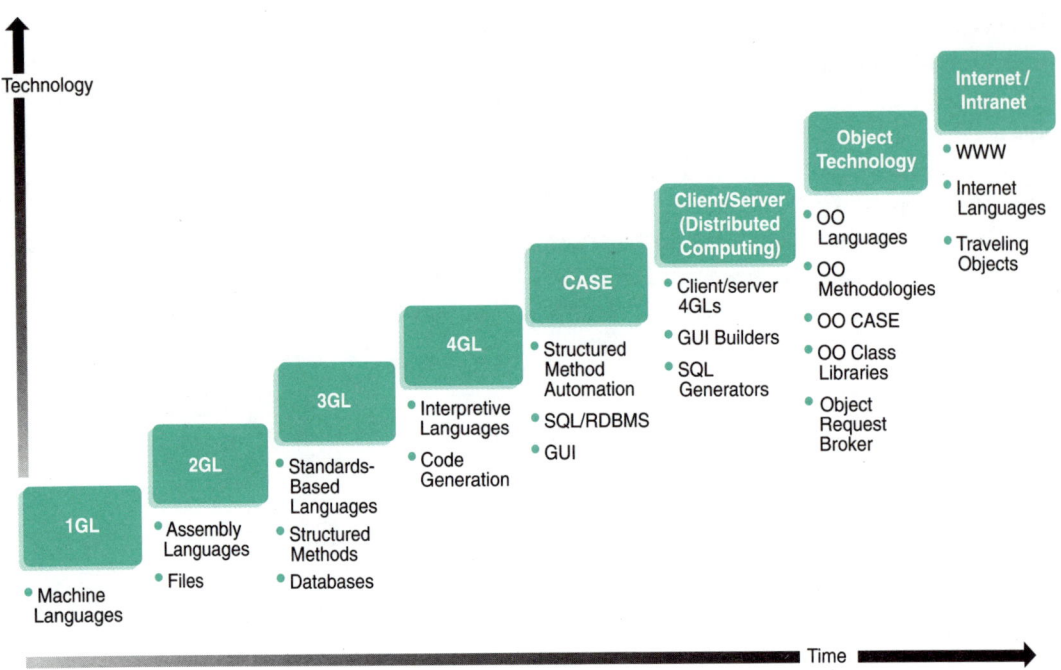

The Evolution of Software Development Technology

This chart isn't intended to mark the precise time a given technology was discovered or introduced, or when its use ended. What it attempts to show is when wider-scale adoption of each technology took place relative to the others. Most of these technologies actually appeared long before there was larger-scale awareness, or use, or commercial availability. Furthermore, most of the technologies introduced in the past are still in use today; and often a new technology or paradigm has its roots in one of the previous phases of evolution.

While all these phases were relevant to and therefore employed by IS developers, some weren't as applicable to technical and embedded software developers. For example, 4GLs, or client/server phases, were less appropriate or significant to developers of embedded software.

Currently, a number of key transitions are in progress. IS organizations are largely offloading applications to the UNIX and PC platforms. The basic form of client and server is the most prevalent. (Typically, the user interface portion of an application is deployed on a PC, and the database or legacy application is deployed on UNIX or kept on a mainframe.) The more sophisticated form of distributed computing, i.e., a network of computing resources with a peer-to-peer relationship, such as distributed online transaction processing (OLTP) and distributed databases are still in the future for most organizations. Few (yet gradually more and more) early adopters in the IS community are piloting object technology and introducing light intranet applications.

Engineers engaged in technical software development (such as operating systems, database management or software development tools), and to a lesser extent, developers of embedded software systems (i.e., the software that is embedded in intelligent devices such as satellites, aircraft, weapon systems, automobiles or your PC) are making a major transition from 3GL and CASE technologies to the object paradigm. Many software vendors are updating their brochures, and in some cases their products, to provide support for the Internet phenomena. It's important to note that objects (and their descendants — i.e., components and Internet applets) are the main catalyst, and are firmly positioned at the center of all these transitions.

So — as you can see, with all these developments, we had quite an interesting and colorful history.

And, yes, clearly, we had *buzzwords!*

In Pursuit of Buzzword Proficiency

Recommended background music for this chapter: "Jabberwocky" from Disney's *Alice in Wonderland*

The Power of the Buzzword

In today's business world, it's sometimes more important for people to *appear* knowledgeable than to *be* knowledgeable. The software industry is buzzword-rich, and it often seems to matter little whether these words are used correctly. CASE. Client/server. GUI. Repository. Class. Polymorphism. The fact is that buzzwords have power, and so do the people who command them (accurately or otherwise). Conversely, if someone doesn't know all the buzzwords, people may think that person doesn't know very much. Many vendors today feel that they have to be *100% buzzword compliant*. For example, it's difficult to find any vendor selling to the IS market who doesn't say "client/server" a lot, regardless of how well he or she understands it.

Key Buzzwords in Software Development History

To explain the buzzwords, let's first glance back at our history and some of the key concepts that relate to our upcoming discussions. We can start with the evolution of the *man/machine interface*, later called the *user interface* and eventually the *graphical user interface (GUI)*. At some point, people began to care about ease of use in their systems and applications. After the short-lived but pervasive *user-friendly* (soon everything from typewriters to ice cream became "user-friendly"), interfaces evolved to the next phase, called *intuitive*. This term meant that one could figure them out without reading hundreds of manual pages — usually. The subsequent phase some call *seductive*, which means that users just can't wait to click on those cute little icons to see what happens. The icons and graphic pictures are designed to seduce people into exploring the system, and (just perhaps) spending more money.

We've recently entered a new phase for user interfaces, which can be called *interactive*. You talk to the machine and it talks back to you. Or it may look at you, or let you look at someone else. Or it can play you a song, or record one of yours. This is certainly amusing, if not tremendously useful.

As I've stated above, one of the most hyped of recent buzzwords is *client/server*. Its rise to fame was gradual. First, we began to use individual PCs; then we connected them together with LANs so we could all share printers or plotters and not have to buy as many. The next stage arrived when people decided that these powerful workstations should actually do some of the processing and execute part of their applications. There certainly were major economic advantages to downloading work from the expensive mainframes to the cheaper PCs, minicomputers and UNIX platforms.

An application can be viewed as a collection of partitions: the user interface, the database or data management, and the application logic. Some of these partitions, such as the user interface, were ideal for residing on the desktop workstation or PC — the *client*. Others, such as the database and data handling code, were ideal for being shared by many users, and thus were placed on a more powerful system such as a bigger workstation, a UNIX platform, or even a mainframe — the *server*. Since an application is divided into several partitions, and since these partitions are distributed across multiple hardware platforms, such applications and their deployment are referred to as "distributed applications" and "distributed computing."

Client/server topology is only one form of distributed computing, but the term is often used (or misused) in the broader sense. Another form of distributed computing is one in which an application's various partitions may reside on several platforms, and the platforms and partitions relate as peers, rather than having one operate as a dedicated server and another as a dependent client requesting a service. For example, a banking application running on a host in one branch may communicate and process transactions together with the same application running on a different host at a different branch. Each host may even have its own clients at its individual branch.

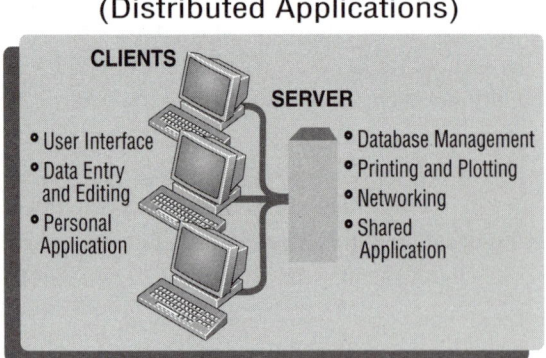

Traditional/Distributed Computing

Repository, which we've mentioned before, is gaining popularity as a buzzword, and rightly so. A repository is a common warehouse where we store all the information related to our applications, and to the development/deployment of those applications, so that developers can share this information.

We can also think of the repository as being like the network that connects all of our telephones together. When we buy a telephone and plug it in, we automatically tie into a network. We can then use that phone to communicate with everyone else on that network. Simple?

The biggest benefit of a repository is *reuse*. (Yes, I know I'm defining a buzzword with a buzzword, but reuse is very important, so we'll keep coming back to it.) Good and productive programmers normally take an old program and modify it to create a new one, which means that they reuse their own software. But nobody else can reuse it. Most experienced programmers wouldn't even consider using someone else's program; they'd be too suspicious that it might not work in a new context, or that it might slow down rather than speed up their efforts. With the repository, everyone develops pieces of software and puts them in, making sure that everything they put in is well defined, operational, debugged and labeled. This way, other developers can build a new program from parts that are already proven and tested. They don't have to take the time to debug, and they have assurance of quality.

The marriage of GUIs and the more common programming languages resulted in another buzzword, *visual programming*, exemplified by Visual BASIC, Visual C++ and others — often used for development of the client portion of an application.

Well, those are some basic software development buzzwords that emerged in earlier times. Now let's move on to the vocabulary of object technology. But before we do that, I need to point out that the term object technology is not interchangeable with GUI. Many applications featuring GUIs aren't based on object technology or the object paradigm. Nor is object technology automatically implied in the notion of visual programming. While icons may correspond to an object, they may not necessarily be implemented in object technology. And, most of all, object technology isn't software development made simple.

In this book I do my best to make the *concepts* of object technology simple, but that doesn't make object-oriented software development itself a simple thing to do. In all honesty, it's not. But, as object technology becomes even more mature and standard-based — allowing us to assemble applications using prefabricated, tested objects — software development will become a lot easier. We must be patient.

Now, on to the object technology buzzwords.

Buzzwords and Object Technology

The scope of object technology is vast and still growing every day. It represents a complete paradigm shift. A *paradigm* is a model, a pattern or a way of doing things. Although it's overused as a buzzword, it still isn't part of most people's everyday vocabulary, so I'm including the definition since even my editorial assistant on this book admits she had to look it up. By a paradigm shift, we mean that we'll be doing things very differently from the way we used to do them. Of course, with new paradigms come new opportunities.

The term object technology can apply to languages, to methodologies, to operating systems, to user interfaces, and to database management systems and repositories. It's not necessary to base every element of an application or software environment on object technology in order to develop software based on the object paradigm. For example, we can use traditional languages and update object-oriented database management systems. No problem. We can use an object-oriented analysis and design methodology while updating an RDBMS. We can do object-oriented programming using *any* procedural language such as C or COBOL. (This does require setting up a certain framework or infrastructure, and establishing coding conventions to ensure compliance to object principles and rules. Most of us would choose to use C++ or Smalltalk which have these constructs built in.) There are many possible permutations.

Here's a quick course in object technology buzzwords, starting with a review of the basics. For examples, I'll refer back to our home audiovisual system from Chapter 1.

Buzzword	**Simple Explanation**	**Example**
Object	An identifiable unit of software	Stereo component
Behavior	Things other objects may request the object to do	Play music
Method	The logic, contained within the object, that implements a specific behavior	Internal electronics
Message	The protocol for communication between objects; the mechanism to invoke behavior	The push of a button, and the device's response to that push

"?????"

That's easy. Now let's make it a little more complicated. Objects are frequently grouped into a *class*. Why? Because people don't want to have to constantly redo everything. Once we've defined the class TV, then we don't need to restate that definition for every specific TV set we encounter. We simply note that the new object, a specific TV set, is a member of the previously defined class TV. We save a lot of time in not having to define the object all over again.

So, classes allow us to group similar objects together so that we can easily share common data and methods with other members of that class. We take advantage of the previously defined information within a class through *inheritance*. In other words, the specific TV set automatically inherits the information for that class that's already in the system. Note also that a change made to that class is automatically propagated to, or inherited by, the subclasses and members of that class. This can also save us time.

Buzzword	**Simple Explanation**	**Example**
Class/subclass	A grouping of similar objects so that the same logic and data can be shared	TVs can be a class; RCA TVs can be a subclass
Instance	A specific object belonging to a class	RCA TV model XL2000 is an instance of the class TVs and of the subclass RCA TVs
Inheritance	The relationship between class and subclass, or class and an instance, by which data and logic are shared (inherited)	An RCA model XL2000 TV inherits all the methods and attributes defined for the class TVs

Every object is an *instance* of a given class. We use the term *generalization* to mean everything about that class; and when we want to be specific, we only need to be concerned with what's different about a particular instance or subclass. For example, if we have a class "employee," we may have a subclass "part-time employee," with the difference being the number of hours worked per week. The subclass still inherits information from the class "employee," so we can still use it to calculate salary or issue an invitation to the company picnic.

Buzzword	**Simple Explanation**	**Example**
Generalization	The common attributes and shared behavior of a class	CD player
Specialization	What's different in the methods and attributes inherited from the generalization class; the ability to redefine the inherited methods	Multi-disc CD player
Encapsulation	The incorporation of data and behavior into an object	Loaded multi-disc CD player or jukebox
Polymorphism	The ability to use the same message to invoke different behaviors, including the acceptance of different types of arguments	Remote control "on" button
State	The status of an object (the value of its attributes) at a given time	The "on" or "off" status of the CD player, jukebox, TV, etc. (The CD player or jukebox can be on, off, playing a song or waiting for input.)

Those two terms "encapsulation" and "polymorphism" may seem a little scary, so I'll explain further. A jukebox plays music using the records inside. Thus, a jukebox is an example of *encapsulation* because all the stereo components (the logic) and recordings (the data) needed to produce music are contained, or encapsulated, within it. One of the most important aspects of object technology is that all the data and behavior associated with a given object are encapsulated within that object. By contrast, in most of today's applications, the behavior of a real-world entity (say, "customer") is buried in thousands of lines of code scattered across several different programs. And the data and attributes of the same entity are hard-coded (e.g., in the Working Storage section of COBOL) or stored in a variety of files or databases. No wonder it takes us so long to implement a change, and even longer to debug it!

A remote control "on" button is an example of *polymorphism* because the same button can be used to turn on both the TV and the VCR. With polymorphism, we use one name and get two or three different types of behavior. Why do we want that? Well, it's convenient, and it makes things easier. Here's another example. Suppose that I (the sending object) transmit a message that says "print." If I send it to one object (my PC), it displays something on the screen. If I send it to another object (my laser printer), it creates a printed paper document. If I send it to another (a plotter), it plots. Polymorphism has made my task a lot easier. I may also pass along arguments (such as "four copies") that invoke more specific behavior.

Note that the remote control "on" button can also be used to cause two different types of behavior from the same object. For example, it can turn the TV on *or* off. The behavior that results is dependent upon the *state* of the remote control (i.e., whether it is in TV or VCR mode) and the TV (whether it is on or off).

Here are some new buzzwords that are currently bombarding the software world. The first is object-oriented *extensions*. There are object-oriented extensions to most common languages, giving us *object-oriented COBOL, object-oriented FORTRAN, object-oriented BASIC* and so forth. Object-oriented programming languages such as C++ (C language with object-oriented extensions!) and Smalltalk contain constructs that directly support the object concepts and terminology introduced in this chapter. Second, things are now becoming *objectified* — which means taking anything we've already got and (rightly or wrongly) giving it an object connotation. This is done to guarantee the all-important 100% buzzword compliance. Our old information engineering methodology becomes *objectified information engineering methodology*. *Component* is another new buzzword that deserves notice. Component can be considered another word for object but with a greater emphasis placed on the reusability of the prefabricated modules and their availability to other software developers. Component terminology is rapidly becoming so popular that it may soon be as common as object terminology. A number of major industry players (including Microsoft) are actively promoting components. Class libraries (a C++ version of a COBOL procedure or a FORTRAN subroutine) are examples of components.

These are the buzzwords of object technology. Some people would call object technology itself a buzzword. Perhaps — it is a new and emerging technology. But the test of a buzzword is permanence. Many terms which were once buzzwords are now a permanent part of our language. Recycling. Database. Online. Others have come and gone. PABA. Cyclamates. Cinerama. Object technology is the way of the future, and you can expect to see and hear these words for a long, long time.

Of course, buzzwords shouldn't be considered a goal in themselves. These words, and the tools and vendors that have come to be associated with them, are only a means to an end. So let's move on to the impact of object technology on you, and on the software community to which you may belong.

Objects, the Software Industry and You

Recommended background music for this chapter:
Sinatra's *My Way*

What It Means to the Industry

Of all the advances in software development technology which we discussed humorously in Chapter 2, few have received so broad an acceptance throughout the computer industry as object technology. I can't think of any major player in the computer industry who isn't in some way involved in the adoption, use or support of it. Every type of software development activity is affected by this new paradigm. We now have object-oriented operating systems, GUIs, languages, methodologies, databases, repositories, frameworks, CASE tools, 4GLs, client/server 4GLs, networking software and more.

Some of these tools and products actually work! Some of them have reached adolescence (i.e., have been successfully used, debugged and enhanced over time). We're beginning to see second- and third-generation releases of object-oriented languages (such as C++ and Smalltalk), methodologies and notation (such as the Object Modeling Technique, or OMT) and object-oriented databases. Industry-specific application software or software packages (such as those designed specifically for manufacturing, accounting, etc.) are emerging in an object form, and vendors of such software are beginning to present object technology as giving them the key competitive edge for their products.

To date, software developers have adopted object technology at different levels and to varying degrees. Technical software developers have been using the object paradigm for several years. Embedded software system developers are also increasingly developing with objects. In general, developers in the telecommunications, computer and financial service industries have been quick to adopt object technology. Elsewhere, among IS organizations, the early adopters in individual companies have been experimenting with or developing objects.

The impact of object technology on the software industry is enormous. Most software vendors have already revamped or are in the process of rewriting their tools and applications in object-oriented programming languages and architecture. Many vendors are increasingly offering object versions of their existing products, thus making the object paradigm highly visible to their end-users who may wish to adopt it.

Once standards and software reusability are in place, the use of object technology will significantly enhance the availability of industry-specific applications and *maintainable* customized solutions. Vendors will be able to offer their customers the option of taking their huge, all-purpose packages apart and selecting only the objects they need. With objects' inherent modularity and loose coupling attributes, along with the ubiquity of the Internet, electronic distribution of software and software fixes will become possible on a much wider scale (using smaller chunks of executable code — i.e., Internet applets).

At that point, the familiar computer outlets that are now oriented toward personal productivity and recreational software products will be able to offer off-the-shelf objects or components for professional software developers as well.

Objects Do It Naturally!

Objects are very important to distributed applications or client/server modes of software deployment. In fact, objects can make the development of distributed applications a lot easier. Why? Well, let's quickly review what this distributed processing trend is all about.

As we discussed in Chapter 3, with a distributed scenario we divide a given application into several partitions — for example, the user interface, database handling and application logic. Often we choose to deploy each partition on a different platform (e.g., the GUI partition on a PC and the database handling and application logic partitions on a UNIX/NT server or mainframe). These partitions communicate with one another by sending messages back and forth, often over a network. It's easy to identify a partition because it has a very well defined role; for example, one partition is responsible for the GUI, one for the database update, one for a payroll application, etc. Sound familiar? Yes, every one of these partitions could be an object. Or it could be a complex object composed of other objects. In other words, an application developed based on objects is distributed-processing-ready, since each object is a partition and can execute wherever we choose on the network. So, with respect to distributed application processing or client/server computing, we can say that objects do it naturally. Picture that on the back of your car!

We're also seeing a lot of new attempts to standardize the way that objects communicate with one another in distributed computing. One of the best known standards is CORBA (Common Object Request Broker Architecture), developed by the Object Management Group (OMG). Microsoft OLE (Object Linking and Embedding) is also emerging as a standard for object-to-object communication. Standards are bound to become a major force in object technology. Someone once said (or should have), "Standards are wonderful because you have so many to choose from!" It's true that multiple standards can be very confusing, but it's because there's such a need for standards that so many people are trying to develop them. Many vendors have also been known to resist compliance and promote "standards" of their own, hoping this will be perceived as a competitive advantage. These are perhaps the reasons why standards typically become established at glacial speed. But in the case of object technology they're evolving much faster, and people are beginning to assert their preference for having a common way for objects to communicate.

What It Means to Your Organization

In praising the virtues of object technology, we've got to admit that we've already increased your expectations. Many people are now expecting object technology to boost productivity 1000%, turn out much better code, be a lot more flexible, and so on. Those expectations should eventually be met — but realistically we know that it's not going to happen overnight. We still need a lot more maturity

"My expectations will be met WHEN???"

in many of the tools, databases and technologies; and developers and organizations still need more experience with them. Reuse won't happen with the first project, or even the second; but if organizations stick to the guidelines they'll start getting reuse with the third or fourth project. In other words, we can expect to reap all the rewards, but just not as fast as some vendors, consultants or methodology gurus would like us to believe.

Identifying the right objects, and designing and developing objects, is not really an easy task. What will become easy is the ability to develop and maintain a software application as an assembly of prefabricated, well tested, off-the-shelf objects. Naturally, in order for the promise of object technology to be fully realized, we must have standards to follow in developing these objects and applications.

For your development staff, embracing object technology won't be easy in the short term. First of all, they aren't used to it. Many of them have spent *too* many years developing applications differently, and it's important to understand how they feel about changing that. Driving an automobile may be a much more comfortable and efficient way to travel than riding a horse, but that automobile is a complex and scary thing to the person who has only traveled on horseback! Besides, some people actually prefer to ride a horse. It can be fun, and it has a certain romantic appeal.

Second, in the short term your developers will be designing and developing both the objects and the application composed of those objects. That's a tall order! Only in the longer term will they be able to develop an application composed mostly of previously developed objects.

To your organization, object technology means that management will have to take on some dramatic new challenges. Object technology is a new way of developing software, and it represents a major change to your entire software development organization. Managers need to take note of this because it's up to them to introduce and manage change.

This paradigm shift is real and will impact your entire organization. But don't let that scare you — eventually, it will also make things *a lot* easier. With object technology, we can finally do things *our way!* All our programming lives we have mimicked the way computers work. Now, thanks to object technology, our computers can mimic the way *we* work, using recognizable, real-world entities. With that, software development becomes a lot less complicated.

So Why is It so Hard to Get Computers To Do What We Want?

Well, probably for the same reason that toasters don't sing, and my cat doesn't write poetry. Computers aren't human. They don't speak our language ... they don't think the way we do ... *and* our software development tools and processes have yet to arrive at the point where they can effectively hide the complexities and peculiarities of computers from the human software developers. Our software development tools and processes were generally designed to mimic the way computers — not humans and our businesses — operate.

To perform tasks, computers need data, and they need programs to access and update that data. That's fine — but in the past we've forced ourselves to translate our real-world concepts into abstract ones such as "data modeling" (which eventually leads to a database) and "process modeling" (which eventually leads to a program) in order to give the computers what they need. And because these abstractions don't correspond to the way people communicate, it was like trying to explain what some transistors do, and some diodes and resistors, rather than what the stereo amplifier does. We had to mold our view of things to somebody (or something) else's level of abstraction — in this case, a computer's, or a methodology's, or some other non-human force.

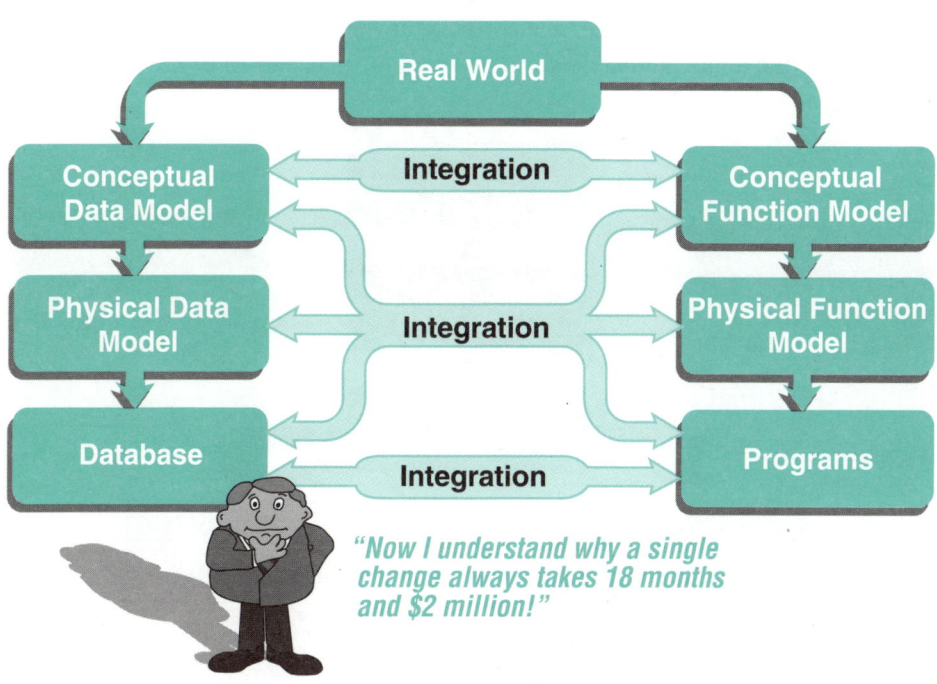

Conventional Approach to Application Development

For example, in a structured methodology such as the Information Engineering Methodology, the above chart would give us the left-hand-side activity, called data analysis, and the right-hand-side activity, called activity analysis, and to keep these two processes in sync with one another we need what's in the middle, called interaction analysis; and we might do some of the activities this month and not get to some of them till six months from now, by which time things will have changed so we'll have to go back and do them over. Whew! I apologize profusely for that long-winded and tangled sentence. Now, I only wish someone would apologize for the long-winded and tangled process. Furthermore, the people who do the data modeling are often in a different department, with different skills and priorities, from those who do the process modeling. The various groups frequently view the world from very different perspectives. Numerous books, methodologies and gurus are available for data modeling, and also numerous — but different — ones for process modeling.

Developing software in this way is difficult because it's unnatural. It's putting the Bloody Mary ingredients in a different binder from the directions. It's having two bartenders and expecting them to cooperate perfectly — and it's expecting the person who updates the ingredients portion of the recipe to stay perfectly synchronized with the person who updates the directions.

Computers may never think the way we do, but with object technology we can interact with them in a manner that's much more natural to us. We're in control. We use objects to represent real-world entities, and then let the technology (i.e., the software development tools) translate them into what the computers need (the applications, databases, screen formats and so on).

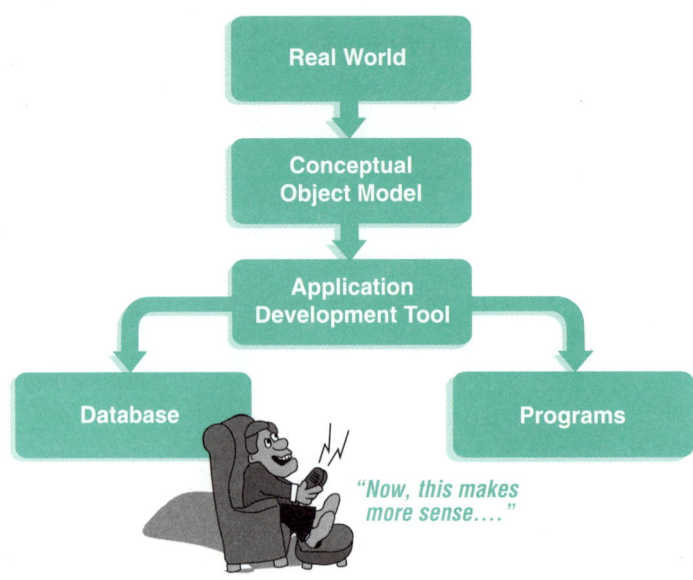

Real-World Representation via an Object Model

36 *Object Technology Made Simple*

Let me give you an example.

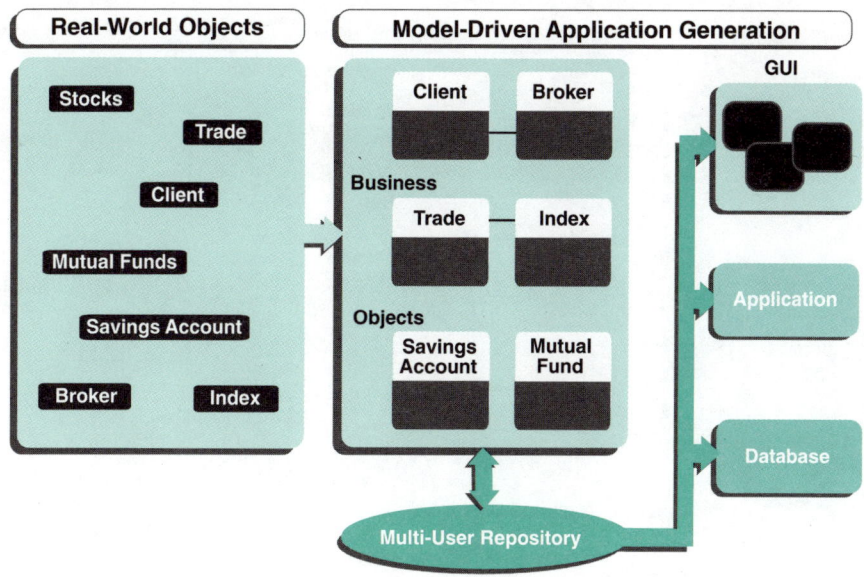

Example: Generating a Real-World Application from an Object Model

The left side of the diagram shows a group of items we see in the real world of investments — stocks, trades, clients, mutual funds, etc. Our objects correspond to these real-world entities, and we can provide information about them with attributes and methods. In this example, we produce a complete model for the desired application, defining all the relevant objects, their behavior (the business rules), their attributes (related data) and the relationship between these objects. Then we can just let the technology automatically translate those models and business rules into what computers need to see — databases, programs and GUIs. Simple? Of course!

We can also look at a similar process using components.

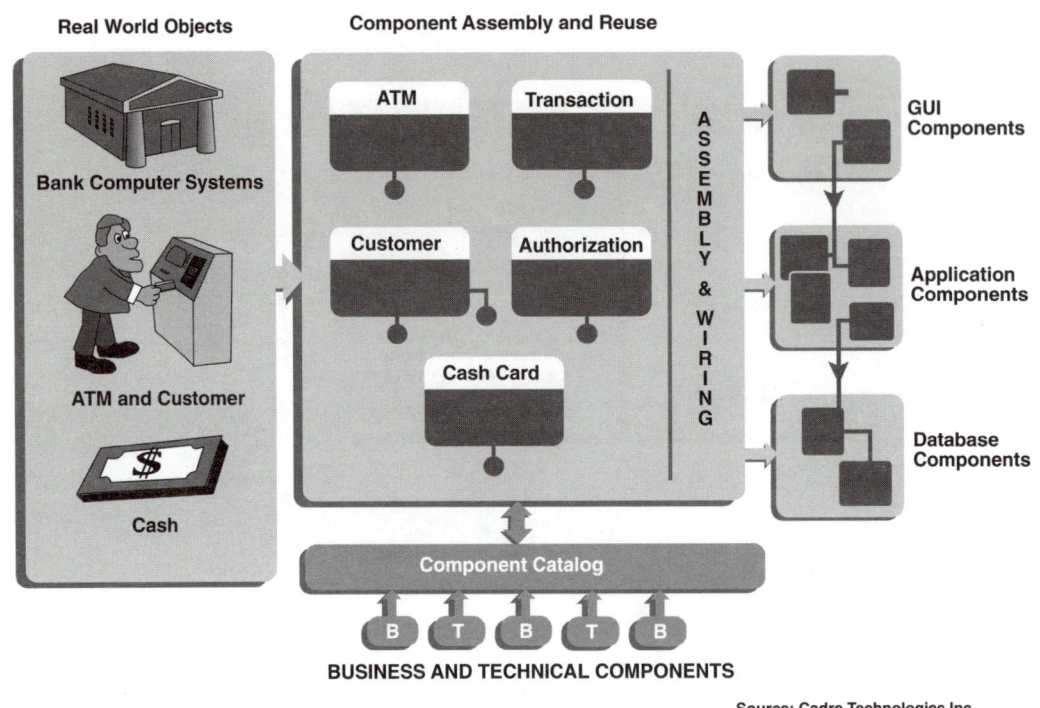

Real-World Example: Component Assembly and Reuse

For every one of the real-world items shown on the left side of this diagram, we can have a component. In this particular environment, the components have connectors (interfaces) so that they can easily be connected (wired) to other components. Each component encapsulates some code or functionality that corresponds to a real-world business object. Now, remember that component development is extremely concerned with reuse, so we're probably going to import other components. We may even want to import some business or technical objects from other developers or vendors to use as components. With component-based assembly and "wiring" (i.e., connecting), we can then produce an application based entirely on reusable components.

A move to object technology promises many changes, some very exciting and others perhaps a little intimidating. However, the benefits in terms of productivity, quality, reduced development time and *working more like humans and less like machines* are taking the software development world by storm, bringing us into the future a lot faster!

People are Object-Oriented ... Programmers are Not! (Yet)

People comprehend and think in terms of objects. And both people and businesses are accustomed to being driven by events. Object software development technology can simply be viewed as an acknowledgment of those facts — and therefore, the paradigm shift to objects is actually a very natural and intuitive one! What makes that shift so challenging is that our experienced software developers and programmers are still more comfortable with the old mousetrap. But that will change.

So, now it's time to roll up our sleeves and develop an object-oriented application — but to do that you need to follow me to a nearby saloon!

5

So Let's Develop an Object-Oriented Application! *(Follow Me to a Nearby Saloon!)*

Recommended background music for this chapter:
The theme from *Bonanza*

Now we're ready to develop an object-oriented application. First we'll define the objects, their behavior and the messages they send to each other, and then we'll write the application itself. And our sample application is — *a bar!*

Identifying the Objects

What kinds of objects do we expect to find in a bar? Well, the most important ones are customers, waiters and waitresses, drinks and bills. Like all objects, each of these has its own areas of concern — for example, the customer is concerned with what he or she wants to drink, the bill, and who the server is. (For convenience, we'll assume one customer and one waiter. Business has been a little slow since Bartender B, on page 7, went out to lunch without mixing the Bloody Mary from the ingredients on the counter.) The waiter's primary concerns are the customer, the bill, the drinks, and, of course, the tip. The concerns of the drink (now we're getting a little bit abstract, but please bear with me) are how it's made, in what kind of container it's served, and how much it costs. The bill is concerned with being totaled, making sure that all the customer's drinks are added in, and being closed out when the customer pays the bill and goes home.

One caution: please note that, by design, I'm going to make everything in our example look easy. In a real-world application, choosing the right objects, identifying what's important about each one, and clarifying the relationships between them won't be so easy. But it will be as rewarding!

"A bar? NOW you've got my attention!"

Object Technology Made Simple 41

Identifying Object Behavior

Now let's look at the behavior of each of these objects. The customer's behavior (assuming he or she is well behaved) is to order a drink, drink it, and pay for it. The waiter's behavior may be to ignore the customer, to step on his or her toes, to take a drink order, to deliver the drink and the bill, and to take the money, not necessarily in that order. What is the drink's behavior? Well, it gets made, and it costs a certain amount of money. A bill's behavior is to include all the drinks the customer ordered, to get added up, and to be closed out.

Defining the Messages

Like objects in any application, these objects communicate by sending messages to one another. The waiter sends messages such as "May I take your order?" or "Would you like to pay your check now?" Sometimes there may be arguments (but not the angry type — this is a civilized bar), such as "Cash or credit card?" Messages from the customer to the waiter might be "Bring me a Bloody Mary," "Bring me my bill," or "Here's the money." In this bar, everyone should be happy, because in object technology the message always includes both the request and the response.

This diagram shows a graphic model of our application with its four objects. In the diagram, the bill sends a message to the drink in order to get the cost information, and the drink responds to the bill so that its cost gets added to the total.

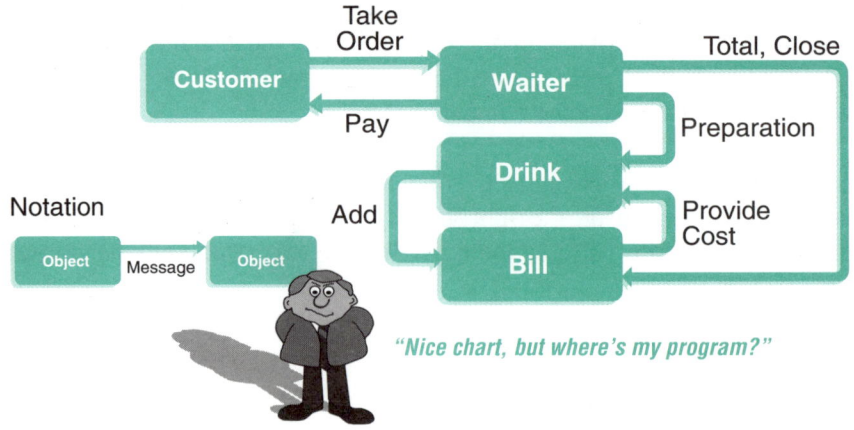

"Nice chart, but where's my program?"

Sample Application: a Bar!

42 *Object Technology Made Simple*

Here's a diagram showing a sample sequence of events and the interactions among the four objects.

1A Customer places order
2A Waiter sends request to Drink
2B Drink is picked up by Waiter
1B Waiter serves Drink
3A Drink asks to be listed on Bill
3B Bill lists Drink
4A Customer asks for Bill
5A Waiter sends request to Bill
6A Bill asks Drink for cost info
6B Bill receives cost info
5B Bill is totalled and picked up by Waiter
4B Waiter presents Bill to Customer and collects
7A Waiter asks to close Bill
7B Bill is closed and Waiter receives acknowledgment

The Objects Interact

Developing the Application

Now that we've defined all the objects and their messages, we can begin the programming. First we write the program that corresponds to each of the four classes of objects, which means coding all the methods and defining all the attributes and data that the instances (objects) in these classes need to function. When that's done, we're ready to write the main program, and we start by defining all the instances of each of the four classes of objects. For example, Jack, Jim and Joe are instances of waiters (i.e., we open a file or invoke an RDBMS table called Waiters). Bloody Mary, Manhattan, Martini and beer are the valid subclasses of the drink class at our bar. Of course, we won't see an instance of the subclass Bloody Mary right away; that isn't created until an individual Bloody Mary has been ordered and prepared.

Object Technology Made Simple 43

Objects, just like people, are *event*-driven by nature — and, just as in the real world, in object technology we need an *event* to make things happen. In this case the triggering event is the customer walking into the bar, so we write a statement for that (e.g., a Wait statement). Subsequently, the messages start getting sent back and forth, and the objects carry out their behavior.

One reminder: We've been using the word "application" in this chapter since it's a familiar notion. But in the pure object world, the application itself is an object. After all, a bar is a real-world object! So is your department, your organization, your company and so forth.

A Real-World Application: Looks Like a Bar!

The notion of drinks and bills carrying out their behavior may seem funny, but this really isn't all that far removed from most business applications. As you can see, we could use the same diagram to represent an order processing system in which the clerk causes the sequence of events to happen. An order processing module interfaces with the factory or warehouse, and the accounting department keeps track of the invoices and payments. The attributes and methods inside these objects are different, but the level of abstraction is the same.

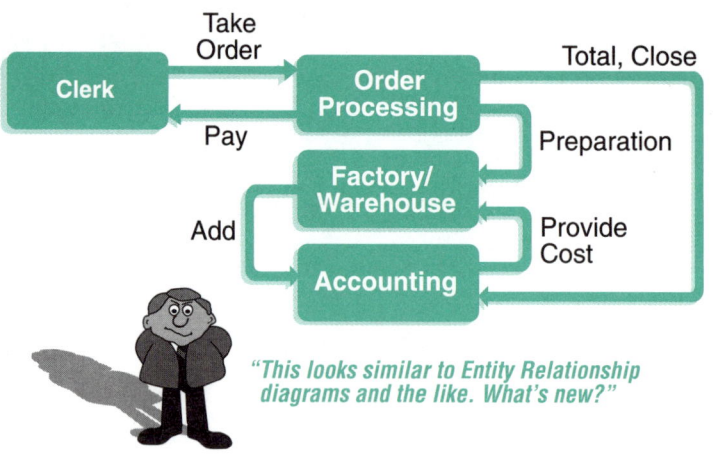

"This looks similar to Entity Relationship diagrams and the like. What's new?"

Real-World Applications... Look Like a Bar!

44 Object Technology Made Simple

Let's Generalize....

One of object technology's greatest advantages comes from our ability to generalize, using what the objects have in common to save us *a lot* of time. For example, we can have an object class called "person" that "includes" the customer and the waiter — and the waitress, and the manager, and the accountant, and a lot of people who don't even go to bars. These are handy, too, because we may want to use the class "person" in another application. We can group all the food and drink into an object called "goods" and then buy that module — already coded, tested and debugged — from an outside source. This same object can be used in our order processing application as well. For that matter, we can create a general class called "business object" which we can also buy off-the-shelf, and define other objects (such as clerk, goods and accounting) as subclasses. These then inherit all that we've defined for "business object." That's the power of object technology: the fact that we can take advantage of previously defined work and only devote our time to the way our particular object (our factory, our accounting department or our policy) differs from that generalization. Instead of starting from scratch, we can simply purchase the code for that general object (e.g., a C++ class library or component) and then just code what makes our particular object different.

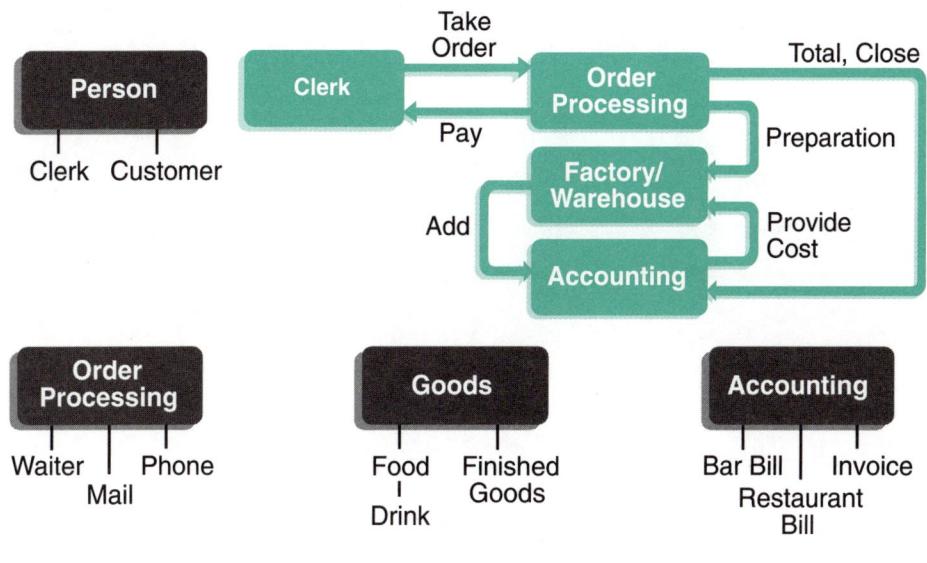

Generalization

The Promise of Object-Oriented Development

In the pure object world, we'll have to do more up-front planning, but *we'll almost never have to start from scratch!* Nearly all the applications we develop will contain common business objects that we can buy, or obtain from someone else, and then customize. What's more, we don't need to learn the entire system. We only need to be concerned with the modules we need to change, and many of them probably won't need to be changed at all. Even if we do need to make changes, we can improve and maintain the code without having to access the source. Software development has just become much less complex. What's more, we don't have to be concerned with what happens inside the objects. That's all been taken care of for us.

For example, today we treat "database management system" as a "black box." We don't need to know how the specific commercial database management system actually organizes or retrieves data, but only what information to give it and what output to expect. If that were true of most of our business objects, imagine the savings in software development time! And with object technology, we have a much better chance at achieving that.

The magic word is *reuse*. The rest of the industrial world has known for centuries that products can be engineered once and then manufactured again and again. *Finally (!)* the same can be said of software — thanks to object technology.

"Hmm…. Reuse! This object technology stuff DOES have some potential!"

Wrapping Your Arms Around Objects *(How to Get Started)*

Recommended background music for the beginning of this chapter: the Pointer Sisters' "So Excited"

Taking that first step into something new is always a challenge. It was probably a little scary the first time you sat behind the wheel of a car, or when you went for that first job interview. For an organization, undertaking a new technology is even more difficult because it's the first step for a lot of different people with a lot of different concerns. But we all know we've got to start somewhere in order to get where we want to go — and, with object technology, the rewards can be compelling.

"How do we go about moving to objects?" you wonder. "How do we sell the idea to our boss?" "Our management is very conservative, and doesn't like risk." The primary reason why organizations are slow to adopt new technologies is that people get set in their ways and resist change. But while the customer in the bar may get up and leave if Bartender B goes to lunch without mixing his drink, some (perhaps wiser) customers will walk around the back to the manager's office and ask that the process be changed. Similarly, a wise manager will listen, since he wants to stay in business, and he'll soon watch his revenues skyrocket when compared to the other bars still using the two-bartender system!

The same is true for the software organizations that are ready to make the changes necessary to adopt object technology — so let's look at how to do it!

How to Get Started with Object Technology

How do you get started? The same way you introduced new processes or tools into your organization before. In brief, you need:

1. An introduction to object technology (reading this book represents the first step here, so you're off to a great start!)
2. The right project
3. The right approach — the right tools
4. Training
5. Mistakes
6. Management and organizational commitment

Object Technology Made Simple 47

Another tall order? Well, perhaps. But some of these (especially item number 5!) are remarkably easy to come by. Let's go through them one by one.

First, you'll need to select the right project for the first use of object technology. It'll be the right project if it's an important and meaningful one; one that's well defined (and well bound) in scope; and one that represents a typical project in your shop. It should also be one that the team understands reasonably well.

Next comes selecting the right systematic approach or methodology for developing an object-oriented application. That isn't difficult — it's just a matter of matching your project and your team to the methodology best suited to them — but it can and should be time consuming. This is a very important step, so take your time and study all the options. Developing in the object paradigm is not like switching from one programming language to another — it requires a lot of up-front planning. (There's more information on methodologies and approaches in the next chapter.)

Once you've chosen an approach, you'll want to select the tools that offer the best support for that approach, and that are well suited to your project and your organization. It's important to understand that selecting an approach (a methodology or technique) and selecting the tools supporting that approach are not really two separate and independent events. Choosing a methodology means paying serious attention to the availability of automated support for it. Furthermore, when you select a tool you're actually selecting a methodology as well, since the approach is inherent in the way the tool can best be used. (More on that, too, in the next chapter.) With the new methodology and new tools comes training, a critical step in the success of that first project. Train, train and retrain till you're sure you're ready to go.

Then, when you feel confident that you're in command of the tools and the methodology, tackle the pilot project. Make mistakes! This is an important part of the learning process, and what you learn from them will benefit your entire organization.

As part of the pilot project, consider showing the end-users a model for the application. Presenting the software as objects helps developers to communicate with end-users in terms of objects; to better identify the objects they should deal with; and to appreciate the advantages of communicating this way with each other! You should also plan to get technical consulting assistance from the growing pool of experienced developers; they can undoubtedly be valuable to your initial design and development efforts.

"This looks like a lot of work. I'm outa here...."

In addition, your success in this initial venture essentially depends on the same elements that made you successful in previous projects. You need to have an accurate understanding of the business requirements and deliverables; a good assessment of the effort required; a capable team; and a solid and realistic project plan.

Finally, to deploy object technology on a wide scale, make sure you have commitment from the management and the "larger" organization. You'll need to put together an infrastructure, a cross-organizational team, in order to ensure an organization-wide commitment to reuse, a common approach, a common toolset, etc. It's through the sharing and the cooperation that you'll obtain the benefits and the rewards of object-oriented development. Remember the five key attributes of object technology: modularity, real-world correspondence, loose coupling, incremental delivery, and, above all, reuse.

You won't get reusability after your first or second project, but you should after your third. You also won't get much benefit from reusability if your project team is the only one producing reusable software! You need the entire organization, and preferably the entire company, to be on the object and reuse bandwagon.

The rest of this chapter is aimed at improving your chances of having a successful experience in adopting object technology.

Smoothing Out the Changes

Here we come to the part that many people find the most intimidating: the changes that adopting object technology will bring to your organization. These changes are sweeping, and I don't want to minimize that. Still, we can try to make them as simple as possible.

The biggest hurdles are, of course, adjusting to a new way of doing things and overcoming people's natural resistance to change. Those hurdles may seem monumental when we're talking about your boss! But don't be frightened. Knowing what barriers you're facing will help you to meet the challenge; and, once you've established a willingness to change, the rest becomes much easier.

Barriers to Adopting Object Technology

To further emphasize our point, we'll depart from the established structure of this book by introducing some new background music in the middle of this chapter.

[Recommended background music for the rest of this chapter: "Tradition" from *Fiddler on the Roof*.]

In guiding your organization toward implementing object technology you'll encounter some resistance. That resistance may come from many directions: your boss, your peers, your team and even other organizations — and the objections will usually relate to five issues: skill, cost, coexistence, performance and control. In software development history, IS developers have faced numerous transitions from one technology to another: from assembly language to COBOL; from batch systems to online; from files to a DBMS; from non-relational databases to an RDBMS; from 3GLs to 4GLs and CASE; and from mainframes to UNIX and PCs — to name but a few. In every instance, there was initial resistance, and some are still resisting.

Here are some of the familiar comments and concerns:

- Skill — "We're a batch shop. We don't know anything about online systems, data communications, etc." "We're a COBOL shop. CASE and 4GL tools aren't for us."

- Cost — "We can't afford to retrain all our people or buy them these new tools."

- Coexistence — "How will this new online system coexist with our current batch systems? We only update our customer file once a week!" "How will this new CASE or 4GL-based application interoperate with our existing system? We can't just throw our current system out!"

- Performance — "But will this COBOL compiler produce code that's as efficient as I can produce with assembly language?" "This RDBMS stuff just can't handle our high volume of transactions."

- Control — "We can't put this system online! Someone can just dial in and corrupt our system! I'd rather just keep the master tape in the vault, right next to the deck of cards that I personally typed for each transaction." "We can't let end-users develop their own applications. They'll create all kinds of silly files and fill up our disk packs in no time!"

Many of these concerns may have had some initial validity, but they often led to some faulty conclusions!

"Ouch! You didn't have to hit so close to home."

Rest assured that you'll encounter some resistance within these five categories. Let me know if you discover any new categories — they'll probably be amusing! Also be assured that, in the same way that the past transitions were inevitable, object technology will eventually be adopted in your organization. This will happen for the same reason that these previous battles were won — *business requirements and competitive pressures will demand it.*

One quick aside: We've explained how resistance to change can be a major barrier to the adoption of object technology. To be fair, we need to acknowledge that the absence of adequate standards, and the slow progress in this important area, is just as much of a barrier. The industry at large must agree to standards before widespread progress can be made.

Management Commitment

Managers are responsible for the orderly introduction of change into their organizations — and it never hurts to let them take credit for that, since they do deserve it! Good managers know that changes must happen. They don't want typewriters on their desks; they want computers. They don't want mimeograph machines around the corner; they want high-volume, high-speed copiers. And if they want the latest, most promising way to develop software, they'll eventually want object technology. At some point they had to make an investment in equipment and training in order to benefit from those computers and copiers, but certainly the benefits have more than proven their worth.

One fact is abundantly clear: adopting object technology is a significant, long-term investment. It involves new tools and services, retraining current staff and recruiting new people. To earn top management commitment and support, we must be able to justify this proposed investment and explain its benefits. As with most investments in technology, the benefits are primarily these:

- Speed — the ability to do our work faster
- Quality — the capability to produce zero-defect software
- Cost savings — the potential to produce the same results using fewer people and resources
- Competitive advantage and innovation — the ability to offer a new product or service; or compliance with government regulation

"If you're looking for somebody to stand in front of your management team and explain all this stuff, call him. Don't call me!"

The fundamental promise of object technology is to allow us to assemble an application largely from prefabricated and well tested parts, as opposed to hand-crafting the entire application every time. Furthermore, the *buy-vs.-build* option is very likely to be the faster and cheaper way every time.

Therefore, depending on which are the key critical success factors for your business, you need to quantify these benefits. Often the potential gains in these five areas may seem modest; and yet, in the balance, they may completely justify the investment in adopting object technology.

I'd also like to think that (ahem!) this book will be helpful in showing your organizations and your management the nature of objects and their potential benefits, in a fashion that's easy to understand, and even fun. I've certainly enjoyed sharing this knowledge with you. Now we come to our promised discussion of methodologies, tools and major players in the field of objects. Check your passport and get ready to do some traveling.

Object Methodologies, Tools and Players

Recommended background music for this section:
Gershwin's *An American in Paris*

The Importance of Modeling

Do you know of very many buildings that were constructed without an architect having first drafted a blueprint for them? Or can you imagine a professional football team showing up for a game without someone having previously drawn up a set of well thought-out plays? Risky propositions, both! If the construction project is important enough, even the landscaping will have been carefully modeled beforehand. In the case of the professional football team, hours and hours of practice may be devoted to rehearsing those planned plays.

But for years we've been developing software without the blueprint, without the model, and without the planned plays or the practice. We'd never travel anywhere by car or by plane if the bridges and aircraft were built that way! We may have gotten away with our reckless software development practices in the past — but, increasingly, the software we develop is far too critical to the enterprise, or to the safe and flawless operation of the aircraft, medical instrument or weapon system. In the previous era of software development (and the present one, in many cases) we could always count on release 1.1 to fix all the bugs we were certain to find in 1.0. But nowadays the software development team that's relying on release 1.1 to fix the bugs in the satellite that's already been launched into orbit is less and less likely to be around for that release!

Having said all that, regardless of whether you're a believer in analysis and design or modeling, *in the object paradigm the need for modeling is paramount*. Object-based development requires a much more sophisticated approach and a great deal more planning than we're accustomed to doing. To handle the complexity of today's applications, to properly develop software based on the new and more sophisticated object paradigm, and to be able to use and produce reusable software, *we must view object modeling as an essential and inseparable aspect of the development process*. This necessity has led to a plethora of object modeling techniques and notations, and analysis and design methodologies and tools. And that will be the focus of this section.

The Methodology Madness!

It's important to understand the various methodologies or techniques and what they can do for us. A *methodology* (a term which some shorten to "method" — but we won't do that, in order to avoid confusion with the word as defined in Chapter 1) is a step-by-step, cookbook-type approach to software development. A software development methodology benefits our projects in several ways:

1. It lets us create a model of the application so that we can better communicate, capture or verify user requirements early.

2. It gives us an orderly process to follow.

3. It keeps everyone following the same guidelines and using a common language and conventions.

4. It can provide a higher level of predictability and therefore repeatability in our development efforts.

5. It helps us to deal more easily with the complexities and difficulties that come along with object-oriented software development.

What's a simple way to explain tools and their associated software development approaches? In Chapter 5, I took you to a saloon to develop an object-oriented application. Now, let's travel a little bit further.

Understanding Methodologies and Tools (Parlez-vous français?)

Let's say you're trying to go from point A to point B — as most people often are. Points A and B can be in any city, state or country you choose; but to make it interesting, in our example, point A is a nice café in the Latin Quarter (*le quartier latin*) on Paris's famous Left Bank, and point B is an elegant (i.e., expensive) and very plush café on the Right Bank, just where the magnificent boulevard Champs Elysées meets the Arc de Triomphe!

Being the strategist and advance planner that you are, you ask the Parisian at the next table how you should get to the café at the Arc de Triomphe. Now, here's where the fun begins. That person could offer you a variety of ways to get there.

The student may draw you a map and show you how to walk there.
The homemaker may point you to the nearest Métro (subway) station.
The businessperson may point to the nearest taxi stand.
The suburban resident may suggest you take the bus.
The tourist bureau employee may advise you to take a guided tour which will certainly stop at the Arc de Triomphe!

In each of these scenarios you may get a map and some additional information, such as directions and descriptions of landmarks or points of reference. In sum, your question gets you your choice of step-by-step approaches (roadmaps) on how to reach your destination. In software development, methodologies give you a step-by-step approach on how to develop your application.

To use the Paris roadmap, you'll need the help of tools — i.e., some form of transportation system (even if you decide to walk, in which case your "tools" are a detailed map and your own strong legs, stamina and patience). Your success with any of these options depends on the availability of subway trains and tracks, taxis, buses, detailed street maps, etc. In software terminology, application development tools provide the automated support that makes using the methodologies practical and effective. The tool vendors are analogous to the transportation services and the map providers. *Without automated support, the methodologies may be of very little use.* For example, the wise guy at the café who suggests you take a chopper (however quick that methodology may be) isn't being very helpful, since there are no convenient take-off or landing areas, and helicopter flights in most major cities are severely restricted.

"I knew it was only a matter of time before you had to show off all your trips to France!"

Object Technology Made Simple 55

There are Many Ways to Get to Point B....

The chosen methodology should also be automated and supported by numerous vendors and experts. The Métro option will get you to the Arc de Triomphe, but it won't help you get from point A to point B in the many areas around the world that aren't served by subway systems.

Some additional observations:

- Every one of the five natives is convinced that he or she knows the best way to get someone from point A to point B (as does the object methodologist!), and all of them are right, from at least one perspective. But you need to figure out which choice is best for you.

- Each methodologist uses a different notation. One uses the Métro map, another uses the bus route map, another uses a street map showing landmarks and shortcuts, etc. — and even these notations are the product of reconciling a lot of previous disagreements. All too often the methodologists argue over just how to draw the Métro map and which symbol to use for a Métro station or a bus stop. Why should we care about that?

- Your decision requires information these natives don't have. For example, only you know:

    - About your physical condition (relevant medical limitations, a healing sprained ankle, jet lag, etc.) and all that luggage you've got to drag with you. The Métro advocate doesn't know that.

    - About how much (or how little) cash you have in your pocket. The taxi advocate doesn't know that.

    - That you're already late for your *rendez-vous* with that outrageously attractive (but impatient) French acquaintance. The walk advocate doesn't know that.

Methodologies often reflect the biases of the methodologists, and they're often devised without a lot of regard for who you are or what your project needs or circumstances might be. These five different options may help you make one short journey today between two points in Paris, but will they work for you next week in west Texas?!

In reality, the tool defines the methodology. The tool is the ultimate dictator of how you get there, and each tool is a unique and different interpretation of the methodology. Individual taxi drivers may choose different routes to get you to the Arc de Triomphe, and none of them may be the route the taxi advocate had in mind. Even with the Métro or the bus system you can get to point B several different ways, choosing the routes and the train or bus lines you prefer.

So, here's the bottom line:

- The choice of methodology and tool should be made simultaneously. They're mutually dependent events, and equally important.

- The characteristics of your project, your implementation environment, and your unique preferences and requirements should drive the decision as to which are the best methodology and tools for you.

- Remember that your objective is to get to point B, not just to collect some nice-looking maps or to ride a Métro line that's clean and quiet (but may be going in the wrong direction!). Albert Einstein said, "Perfection of means and confusion of ends seem to characterize our age." Let's not live up to his expectations.

One caution — These days there's a lot of hype about software development techniques and their notations, and some vendors may distort these things in order to sell their products. Don't be taken in by a smokescreen of buzzwords! Having a common approach and a practical methodology is what's important, not the notation and the compliance with a snapshot of some guru's academic sentiments at a particular moment in time. If a guru or a vendor spends a lot of time talking to you about the purity and the importance of a notation, you might want (just this once!) to quote my shadow personality's comments at the bottom of the page.

Evaluating the Methodologies

The following table lists some of the better known object-oriented development techniques. I've included an aerial view of each one's popularity (i.e., how well known, how widely published and how heavily used it is) and its relative tool support, plus some specific observations.

"It's not the notation — it's improving developers' productivity, Sherlock!"

Object-Oriented Methodologies Made Simple!

Methodology or Technique	Popularity (Level of Usage and Awareness)	Availability of Tools (Automated Support)	Comments
OMT (Object Modeling Technique)	High	High	Wide variety of applications (IS, technical software, embedded software)
Martin-Odell	Low	Very limited	Information engineering bias
Shlaer-Mellor	Low	Limited	Embedded software bias
Booch	Low	Limited	
Jacobson	Very low	Limited	The Use Case feature of this approach is currently being adopted and incorporated into various tools
Coad-Yourdon	Very low	Very limited	
Wirfs-Brock	Very low	Very limited	Smalltalk bias

You can see that OMT, the Object Modeling Technique, is emerging as the apparent choice of most developers. As the most popular methodology, it's widely automated, with many vendors offering tools in support of it. The competition among these vendors keeps the tool support constantly improving and the costs in balance, much to the advantage of developers.

What's important to know about methodologies is that each is best suited to a specific type of project — long term vs. short term, large development team vs. small group, rush to market vs. having zero defects, etc. Preferences as to degree of formality and rule structure also play a part in selecting a methodology. Different scenarios require different approaches! Still, when selecting a methodology, some basic criteria always apply:

1. Make sure that it's widely published. There should be a lot of books available to explain the approach, and a lot of people who have answers when you need them.

2. Make sure the methodology you choose is widely automated, so that many tools are available to support it.

3. Play it safe! Pick a methodology that's been widely tested and has proven its worth. Continuing popularity and wide support are good metrics for this.

If only one vendor automates the methodology, stay away from it. Ditto if only one small group understands it. If both the small group and the one vendor work out of the same shop, then steer clear! Take your time and review all the options; then choose the methodology and the tool that are right for your project and your organization.

Who Are the Big Players in Object Technology?

Here's a list of the key players in the large and crowded object development tools market. Only the market-share leaders and their specific areas of leadership are presented here. If you're a vendor with market-share leadership in an important area and feel that I've unfairly left you out, please forward your profile and your claim to fame (along with a bottle of Chateau LaFitte 1975 or equivalent) to my attention! I'll give them my utmost consideration for the next revision of this book.

For a less biased (and please note that I said "less biased" and not "unbiased") evaluation of tools, methodologies, vendors, trends and more, you can also seek advice from a plethora of industry analysts and resources. Gartner Group (I look to them for qualitative information), IDC (International Data Corporation, for more quantitative information) and DATAPRO Information Services Group (for vendor and product profiles) are some of the larger and more established ones.

"You vendors always talk about yourselves!"

Key Players in Object Technology Made Simple!

Leader	Areas of Leadership
Borland	C++/Pascal programming tools
Cadre*	Object model-driven tools (OO CASE); component assembly and reuse
Centerline	C++ programming tools on UNIX
Digital (DEC)	Communication between distributed objects; CORBA-compliant Object Request Broker implementation
Hewlett-Packard	OO framework and development environment
IBM	C++ and Smalltalk programming environment on OS/2; language-independent OO framework
Microsoft	Programming tools (Visual C++, Visual BASIC); enabling technology for components — OLE (Object Linking and Embedding)
NeXT	OO operating system and development environment
Object Design	OO DBMS
OMG (Object Management Group)	The key body, composed of users, vendors and consultants, that seeks to establish and promotes the use of standards related to object technology
ParcPlace-Digitalk	Smalltalk programming tools; visual development tools
Rational	Ada programming tools, methodologies and methodologists
Rogue Wave	C++ class libraries
Sun	Distributed objects development environment; Java programming tools
Sybase/Powersoft	OO client/server 4GL
Visix	OO cross-platform development environment

---

* At the time of this writing, Cadre Technologies Inc. and Bachman Information Systems, Inc. are in the process of merging. Pending approvals, the new company will be known as Cayenne Software Inc.

Well, we've traveled through history and around the world to examine the state of software development technology today. Now, here's a new and challenging question: what does the future hold? Chapter 8 offers some intriguing insights.

What Lies Ahead?

Recommended background music for this chapter: "Tomorrow", from *Annie*

The object technology revolution may someday be compared to the way integrated circuits (ICs) revolutionized the electronics industry. The development of ICs resulted in a virtual technology explosion — VCRs, musical synthesizers, microwave ovens, camcorders, PCs, cellular phones, and hundreds of other electronic gadgets that we see everywhere. Suddenly, so many ICs were available that we could practically design a new gadget overnight! But in order for this to happen, a middle step had to occur: the establishment of standards.

Early on, the electronics industry embraced the notion that ICs had to be standardized so that they could be plugged in here, or plugged in there, and still be guaranteed to work with the rest of the product. Rather than balking at the need to conform to standards, the engineers welcomed them, knowing what it would mean to the future of their industry. Now we need such standards for software objects. That won't be easy, especially considering the software industry's well known resistance to change — but it must happen. It's the direct road to the future.

With the standardization of software modules should come the *application explosion*. Standard software objects, with literally millions of uses, should open the door to a tidal wave of applications we can only begin to imagine; and that application explosion will have ripple effects throughout all of industry. All of the industrial world — in fact, all of the world — could reap the benefits! We're standing on the threshold of a tremendously exciting age, and you can expect our generation of software developers to truly make history. This is the inevitable (and wonderful!) result of all that has led us to this point.

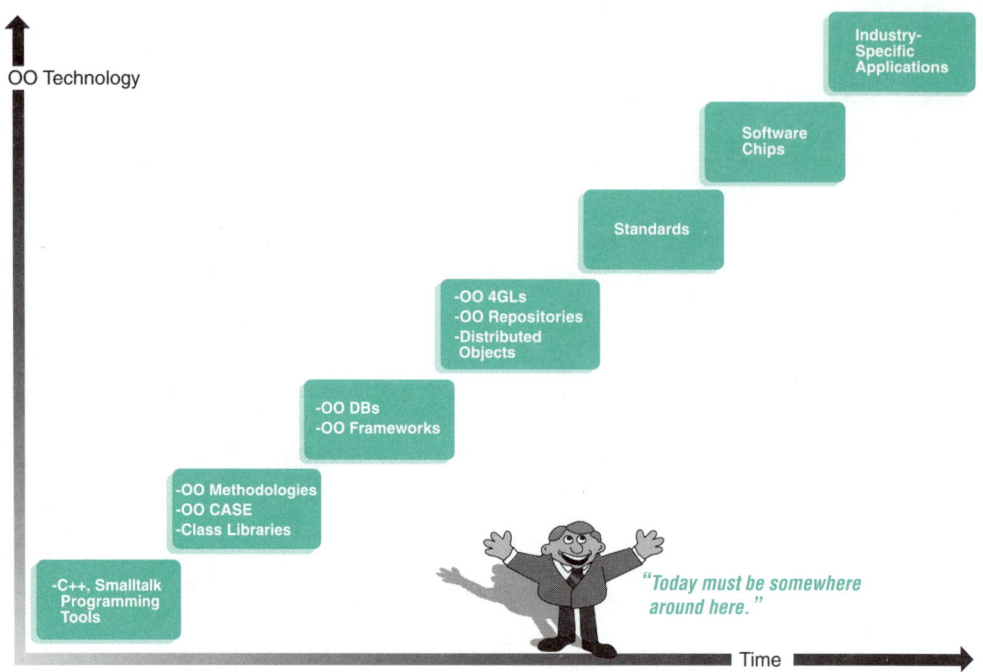

The Evolution of Object Technology

Object technology has been evolving very rapidly indeed! First came the object-oriented languages, followed by programming tools and environments. Next, a number of books on object modeling techniques and methodologies were published and/or popularized. These were quickly followed by automated support in the form of CASE tools. After some use of these new programming languages in real-world projects, the need for some basic (C++) class libraries, object databases and development frameworks became apparent. We're now beginning to see the emergence of 4GL tools that support object-oriented constructs, and repositories that support object tools and provide for object storage and retrieval. Increasing functionality also allows us to place, locate and access objects across a network.

Although significant progress has been made toward establishing standards for the use and deployment of the object paradigm, a lot of work still remains to be done in this area. Establishment of — and an industry-wide commitment to — standards is the primary prerequisite to having commercially available, bulletproof, reusable software components — veritable "software chips." Eventually, though, these software chips will emerge, setting the stage for an explosive growth in the availability of industry-specific applications and turn-key solutions that we can all license and customize to our unique and exact business requirements.

The software development of the future may resemble the picture shown here.

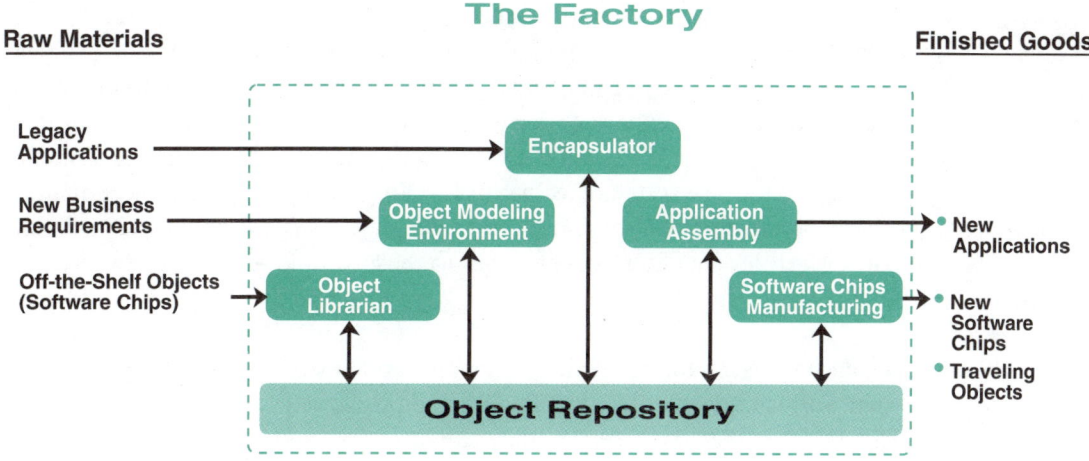

Software Factory of the Future

The main priority of software development organizations in the future will be exactly what it should've been in the past: understanding and responding to business requirements. However, the way in which these new applications will be developed will be different. Developers will assemble an application mostly from previously developed components, with a few components customized to fit the precise requirements. Very few specialized vendors and developers will actually develop objects, while many more will assemble the reusable, commercially available components to create applications and products. The object repository will serve as a warehouse where we can store, manage and retrieve externally acquired software chips as well as encapsulated (component-ized) legacy applications and business rules. The "traveling objects" mentioned in the above diagram, by the way, are Internet-aware objects that can travel from site to site providing well defined services.

"How entertaining! Let me see… When making long-term predictions, it's more important to be interesting than accurate! Right?"

Object Technology Made Simple 65

And Finally, the Conclusion....

Object technology promises to transform the software development process from a complicated art form to a much more manageable, repeatable, modern manufacturing-like process. It also has the potential to provide us with a still higher and *more natural* level of abstraction where we can state and meet our business needs through computers and automation.

Like many new technologies, objects will eventually become a pervasive part of our existence without our realizing it. Objects are already embedded within many of the products and technologies we buy; and we don't need to be object experts to derive the benefits that they offer an organization. On the other hand, let's not forget that it's people, and not tools, methodologies and technologies, that develop applications. No tools or software technologies can make up for poor project planning and judgment, questionable development practices, or inadequately trained or skilled personnel. Tools and technologies offer the maximum benefit only to those who know how to deploy them properly.

And finally, object technology is not the destination; it's only another stop in our journey toward the utopian scenario where software development technology and computers are totally invisible and transparent to us. That is, when they can see us ... they can hear us ... and they can understand *our* natural language. And, remember, as Sydney J. Harris said, "The real danger is not that computers will begin to think like men but that men will begin to think like computers." Perhaps object technology will play a major role in ensuring that we don't.

Happy object developing!

"Whew! I thought he'd NEVER end! Y'know, just between us, nobody is happier than I am to see this book end. I must say I'm amazed that you actually made it all the way to this page. Personally, I started having some long blinks midway through the third chapter! Well, friends, I wish you all the best in your future software development projects. May there be no unidentified objects flying around your shop! I've enjoyed interrupting your reading and talking to you.

"Please keep in touch! If you'd like to chat some more, you can reach either one of us at 104027.2243@compuserve.com. If I'm too busy, I'll have him get back to you."

Index

3GLs, 15-16, 20, 21
4GLs, 17, 20, 31, 50, 64
2001 — A Space Odyssey, 13, 17

Activity analysis, 36
Alice in Wonderland, 23
Also Sprach Zarathustra, 13
An American in Paris, 53
Annie, 63
Approaches, object-oriented. *See* Methodologies
Arc de Triomphe, 54-58
Assembly language, 15, 20
Attributes of object technology, 2-5, 49
Awakening, the, 14-15

Bachman Information Systems, Inc., 61, 75
Bahar, Mory, 75
Bar (as an example), 41-45, 47
Behavior of an object, 9, 26, 42, 44
Bloody Mary, 6-7, 36, 41, 42-43
Bloody Mary recipe, 6, 73
Bonanza, 41
Booch methodology, 59
Borland, 61
Business (in driving software development), 13-14, 51, 65
Buzzwords, 11, 21, 23-30, 58

C language, 15, 26, 29
C++ language, 19, 25-26, 29, 31, 45, 64
Cadre Technologies Inc., 38, 61, 75
CASE, 6, 18, 20-21, 23, 50, 64
Cayenne Software Inc., 61, 75
Centerline, 61
Champs-Elysées, boulevard, 54
Chen, Peter, 16

Class, 23, 27, 43, 45
Class libraries, 20, 29, 45, 64
Client/server, 18, 20, 21, 23-24, 31-32
Coad-Yourdon methodology, 59
COBOL, 15, 26, 29, 50
Common Object Request Broker Architecture, 33
Components, 21, 29, 38, 45, 65
Computer-Aided Software Engineering. *See* CASE
Constantine, Larry, 16
Contemporary Period, the, 18-19
CORBA, 33
Coupling, loose, 2-4, 49

Data analysis, 36
Data dictionaries, 17
Data modeling, 35-36
Database management systems. *See* DBMS
DATAPRO Information Services Group, 60
DBMS, 17, 26, 46, 50
DEC, 61
Delivery, incremental, 2-5, 49
DeMarco, Tom, 16
Digital, 61
Dijkstra, Edsger, 16
Disney, Walt, 23
Distributed computing, 20-21, 24, 32, 64
Dvorak, Anton, 1

Einstein, Albert, 58
E-mail (as an example), 8
Employee (as an example), 10, 28
Encapsulation, 28-29, 65
Events (as triggers for action), 39, 44
Evolution of software development technology, 13-21

Object Technology Made Simple 69

Expectations, user, 13, 33
Extensions, object-oriented, 29

Factory (as an example), 8-9, 44-45
Feudal Times, 15
Fiddler on the Roof, 49
FORTRAN, 15, 29
Fourth-generation languages. *See* 4GLs

Gartner Group, 60
Generalization, 28, 45
Gershwin, George, 53
Getting started with object technology, 47-52
GUI, 20, 23, 25, 31-32, 37

Harris, Sydney J., 66
Hewlett-Packard, 61
Home stereo system (as an example), 2-5, 26, 35
How to get started with object technology, 47-52
HTML, 19

IBM, 61
ICs, 13, 19, 63
IDC, 60
Incremental delivery, 2-5, 49
Inheritance, 27
Instance, 27-28, 43
Integrated circuits, 13, 19, 63
International Data Corporation, 60
Internet, 19-21, 32, 65
Internet/Intranet Era, 19

Java, 19
"Jabberwocky", 23
Jacobson methodology, 59
Key attributes of object technology, 2-5

Latin Quarter, the, 54
Level of abstraction, 14-15, 17, 66
Loose coupling, 2-5, 49

Machine language, 14-15, 20
Machine part (as an example), 10-11
Management commitment, 49, 51-52
Martin-Odell methodology, 59

Message, 7-11, 26
Method, 7-11, 26
Methodology, 16-17, 48, 54-60
Métro, Paris, 55-58
Microsoft, Inc., 29, 33, 61
Mistakes, 47-48
Modeling, 53
Modern Times, 19
Modularity, 2-5, 49
"My Way", 31

New Frontier, 19
New World Symphony, 1
NeXT, 61

Object, definition of, 6, 7, 26
Object Design, 61
Object Management Group (OMG), 33, 61
Object Modeling Technique (OMT), 31, 59
Objectification, 29
OMG, 33, 61
OMT, 31, 59

Paradigm, definition of, 25-26
ParcPlace/Digitalk, 61
Paris, 54-58
Part (as an example), 10-11
Pointer Sisters, the, 47
Polymorphism, 23, 28-29
Process modeling, 35-36

Rational, 61
Real-world correspondence, 2-5, 49
Renaissance, the, 16-18
Repository, 24-25, 31, 65
Reuse, 2-5, 25, 29, 46, 49
Rogue Wave, 61

Shlaer-Mellor methodology, 59
Sinatra, Frank, 31
Smalltalk, 26, 31, 59, 64
"So Excited", 47
Specialization, 28
Standards, 32-33, 51, 63-65
Star Trek, 17

State of an object, 28
Stereo system (as an example), 2-5, 26, 35
Strauss, Richard, 13
Subclass, 43-45
Sun Microsystems, Inc., 61
Sybase/Powersoft, 61

Third-generation languages. *See* 3GLs
"Tomorrow", 63
"Tradition", 49
Training, 47-48
Traveling objects, 20, 65

Use Case, 59

Vacuum tubes, 13
Visix, 61
Visual programming, 25

Wirfs-Brock methodology, 59
Wiring of components, 38
World Wide Web, 19-20

Yourdon, Ed, 16

Recipe for a World-Class Bloody Mary!

Ingredients:

4 oz.	Crushed ice
6 oz.	Tomato juice
1-1/2 oz.	Lemon juice
1 tsp.	Worcestershire sauce
4 dashes	Tabasco sauce
1 tsp.	Minced horseradish
2 oz.	Vodka
1/8 tsp.	Salt
1/8 tsp.	Freshly ground pepper
1/8 tsp.	Minced garlic
1	Celery stalk
1	Lemon slice

Directions:

Mix the tomato juice, lemon juice, vodka, horseradish, garlic, ice, worcestershire and tabasco sauce. Add pepper. Add salt to taste. Shake well. Strain and pour into a tall glass. Insert celery stalk. Add lemon slice on rim and serve.

Source:
Object Technology Made Simple
by Mory Bahar

About the Author

Well known to software development audiences around the world for his delightful "made simple" approach and his ready wit and humor, Mory Bahar is an authority on software development, an author and a frequent speaker on object technology. As Vice President of Marketing and Professional Services at Cadre Technologies Inc.*, he led the company's successful effort to become the leading provider of object modeling products and services worldwide (as acknowledged by International Data Corporation and Gartner Group for several years).

Before joining Cadre, Mory was the top marketing executive for the Software Products Group at Unisys Corporation, where he was the driving force behind the company's application development framework. He began his career in the IS organization at Burroughs Corporation, where he led the project team that created the online architecture and standards that enabled rapid development and deployment of the next generation of internal systems. He holds a BS degree in Electrical Engineering from the University of Texas and an MS degree in Computer Science from the University of Illinois.

Mory describes his favorite pastimes as traveling, aerobics, downhill skiing, winning at blackjack, making noise with his guitar, playing on the computer with his six-year-old daughter Nina, and, of course, good Bloody Marys.

---

* At the time of this writing, Cadre Technologies Inc. is in the process of merging with Bachman Information Systems, Inc. Pending the necessary approvals, the new company will be known as Cayenne Software Inc.

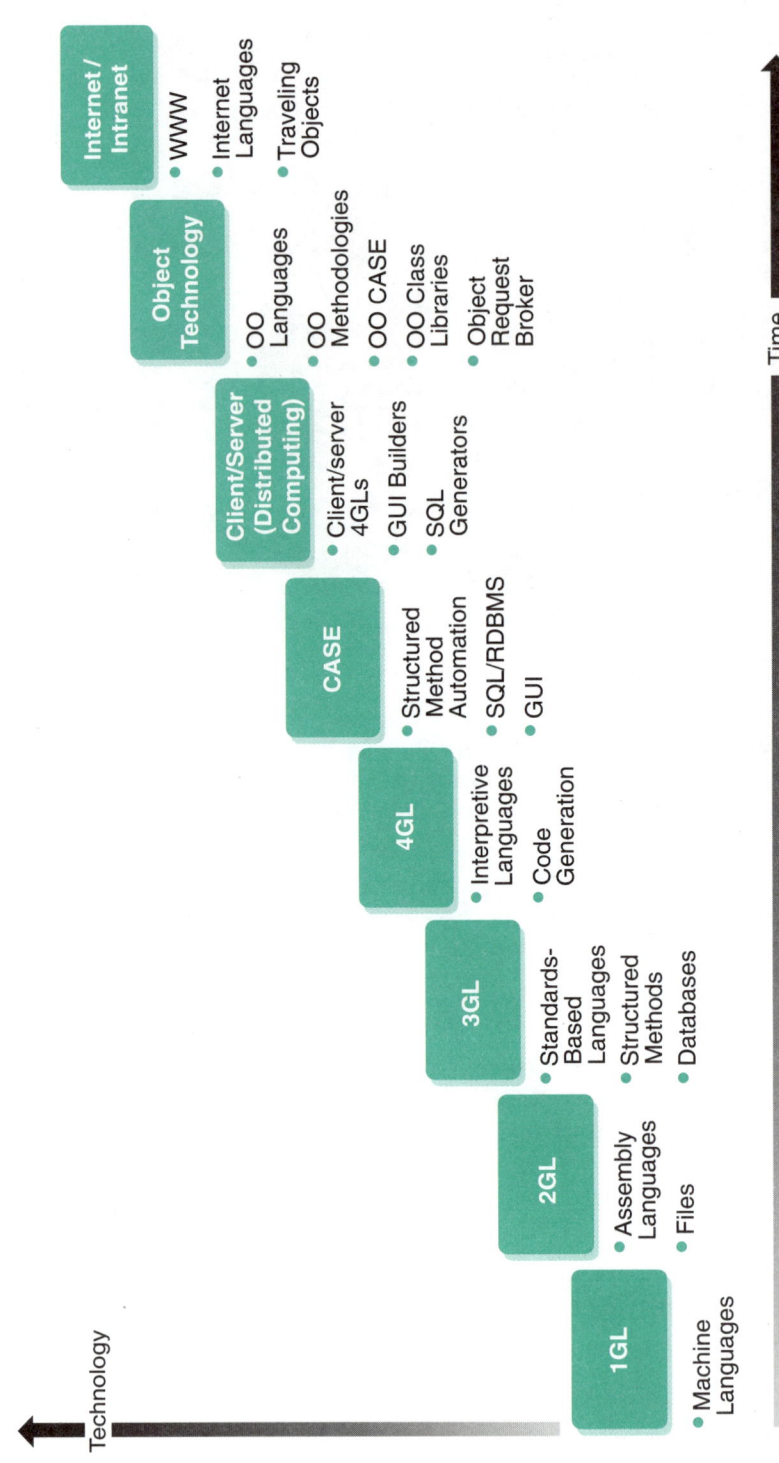

The Evolution of Software Development Technology

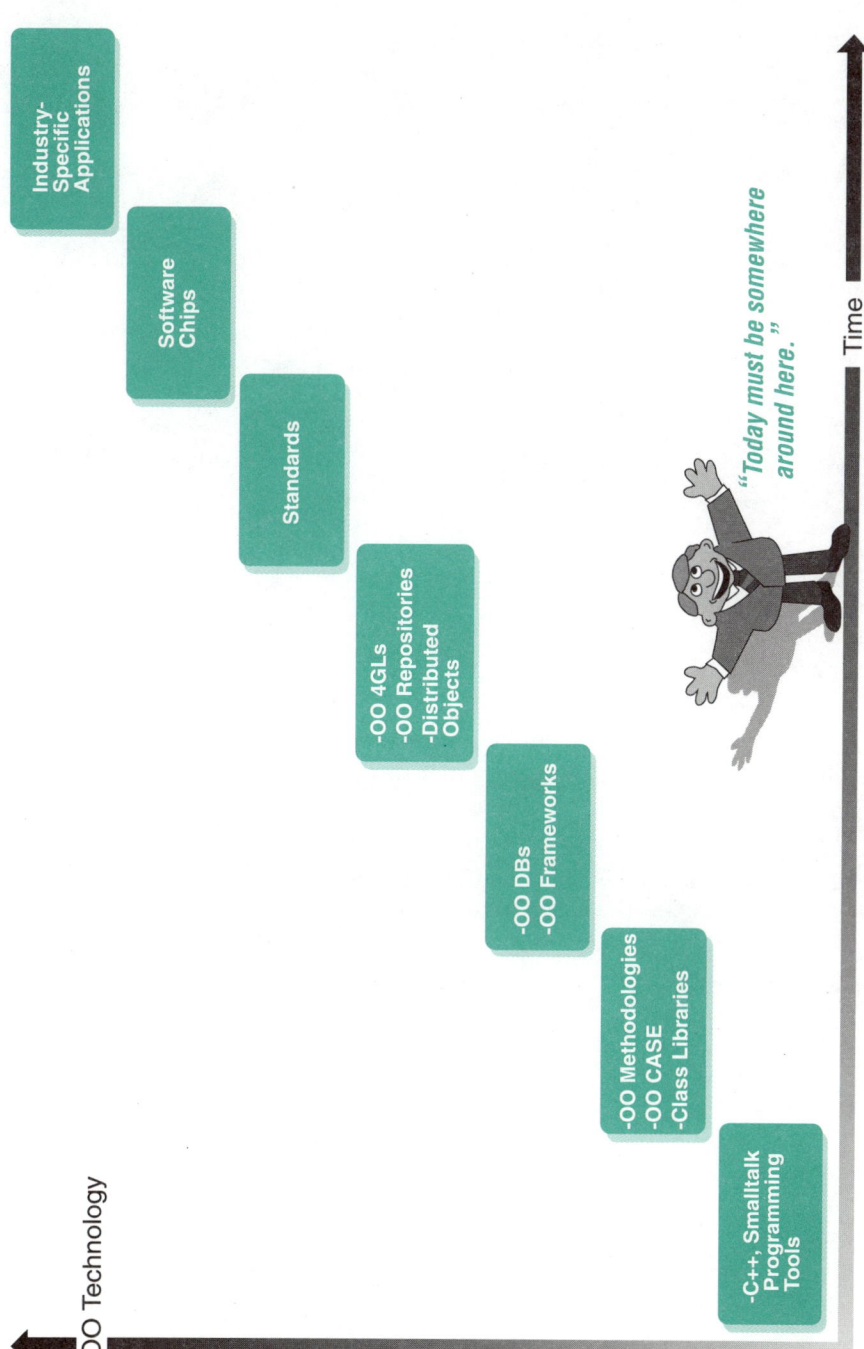

Ordering Information

This book is available from authorized distributors, or may be ordered directly via e-mail (104027.2243@compuserve.com) or mail:

Mory Bahar
Simple Software Publishing
2220 Middle Road
East Greenwich, RI 02818
U.S.A.

Please include a personal check, money order or purchase order number as appropriate.

Volume discounts are available for quantities greater than twenty.